Mabu
Mabu

Nornie
Bero

Mabu Mabu

Nornie Bero

An Australian Kitchen Cookbook

Hardie Grant

BOOKS

Acknowledgement

I would like to acknowledge my cultural heritage and
pay respect to my Ancestors of the Komet Tribe of the
Meriam People of Mer Island in the Torres Strait.

I also acknowledge the Traditional Owners of the land
on which my businesses are based and where the book
was developed in Naarm (Melbourne), the Boonwurrung
and Wurundjeri Peoples of the Kulin Nation, and I pay
respect to their Elders past and present and emerging.

This book celebrates the many Aboriginal and Torres
Strait Islander communities who have been gathering,
growing, harvesting and using native ingredients for more
than 60,000 years on the lands now known as Australia.
Sovereignty was never ceded.

www.mabumabu.com.au | @mabu_mabu_aus
@propriltor: nornie bero

Part One:
The Beginning

I'm an Island girl, from Mer in the far east Torres Strait, at the most northern point of Australia, in between Papua New Guinea and the tip of Cape York. I'm from the Komet People – that's our tribe, and Wanpun, which is a gecko – that's my totem.

My father's name was George, or Gai. He met my mother, a Dutch-Jewish traveller, in a nightclub in Far North Queensland when he was only twenty, and by the time I was eighteen months old, Mum had left and Dad was raising me on his own. Soon we moved to Moa, a bigger island closer to the mainland with two communities: St Pauls and Kubin. On Moa, everybody knows everybody. It's the 'Island Wireless', as we call it.

From the youngest age, I was part of the working household: growing produce, weeding and cooking. My earliest memories are of Dad teaching me how to make damper when I was barely able to see over the stovetop. To raise extra money, he started a tuckshop on one side of a bamboo wall running down the middle of our house. After running the tuckshop each day, he would go off to his council job picking up the sewerage from the houses on the island – not the most pleasant job! There was no running water, so everyone had a thunderbox. But he made me understand what hard work really was.

Every morning I'd wake up when it was still dark and help Dad make pumpkin buns that I would deliver to the locals before school.

He paid me in marbles, too. Island kids are ruled by marbles – I had a milk tin full of them! Milk up north is always powdered, by the way; it was a long time before I knew fresh milk even existed. Every month, a barge would hit the wharf loaded with supplies – powdered milk, sugar, flour – and everything would get snapped up. Apart from those few basics, everything came from the island. We grew our own vegetables, fished every day and learned the circle of life.

Growing up with a spear in my hand seems unreal, but that was my beginning. Dad made me my own spear and if it ever got bent out of shape, I'd have to fix it myself. Before the sun rose, we would head out to the reef holding a kerosene lamp for a torch to catch anything that had been trapped in the lagoons overnight. I remember trying to spear octopus before they slithered away, or finding a giant clam, ready to cook in coconut milk. The creamy, sweet taste of coconut always makes me remember my aunties and grandmothers sitting in their colourful aw gemwalies (Island dresses), moud merring (gossiping) with big smiles and koquam (hibiscus) flowers in their hair. They would skin yams and

scrape coconut with a madu (a wooden board
with a metal edge), and prepare banana leaves
to wrap damper and fish, all while singing our
traditional songs.

When I hit double figures we moved again,
to Horn Island, and I would ferry over to school
on Thursday Island, the capital of the Straits.
Dad was starting to get sick with arthritis,
and I had the responsibility of looking after him.
I would go out catching big fish from the wharf
for us to eat. We'd scoff oysters from the rocks as
a snack, or pick up mikeer fruit that had dropped
onto the sand, cracking open the seed to find a
silky rolled sea almond inside, then wash it down
with wongai (Island plum) picked straight from
the trees. Delicious.

By his mid-thirties, Dad was really unwell
and could no longer work. For someone
as vibrant as he was, it was hard to watch.
Eventually he arranged for me to be billeted
out for high school, first to Cairns and then
Townsville. It was a big shock to come to
mainland Australia, but I discovered I had an
amazing relative, Grandma Aba, who would
change my life forever.

Grandma Aba was a legend. She had a halfway house in Townsville for kids who had come down from the Islands, and it was here that I finally had my own room. Grandma Aba was actually Dad's dad's sister – I never met my dad's parents because they died when he was fifteen – but she was like my real grandma. She was a very Christian lady and we had to get dressed for church every Sunday. Living at her home on Garden Street was like being back on the Islands; it had a full Island garden. There were huge fruit trees – mango, sorbee, bell fruit – growing tall over the house. Grandma Aba would send me down to the local milk bar with a note written in the most perfect running writing to do 'book up', which was to shop for groceries on her account. There were no sweets or chocolates; she wasn't a treat lady. You had to work hard for treats. She also had tonnes of cats – at least five – and when the cats would have kittens anyone who came round would be offered one.

Breakfast was always at the same time – if you missed it, you didn't have it! And if you came home after dinner, then you'd be making your own. Sometimes I'd come home late, but I had been out fishing for hours. I would just throw the line in from the wharf and catch squid and garfish. It's easy to forage for food in Townsville – there are trees full of five-corner fruit (starfruit) right there on the side of the road, and we'd eat them by the bucketload. I went back up north for Christmas recently and my cousin said: 'Pull over here!' And she made me get out and climb a tree to pick the five-corner fruit. I was thinking, 'I'm in my forties, I shouldn't be climbing trees – how will I get down?' And my cousin said, 'I just wanted to see if you would do what I told you.' I was scratched from head to toe and there was my cousin laughing at me. But at least we had plenty of starfruit.

22

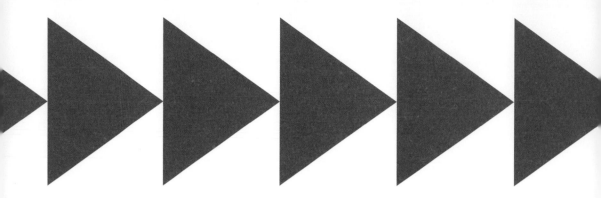

You know I failed cooking at school? My home economics teacher actively disliked me. We were doing sewing, and kids' cooking, but I wanted to build stuff and do things with my hands. At school I was more of an athlete, not an academic. The choice was between finishing high school or going to work. Half of my friends joined the army at the end of Year 10 and the only reason I didn't do it was because Dad wasn't around to give me the permission slip. I moved again, to Innisfail, and started working on farms. I was only sixteen, and would drive around picking up the farm workers, take them to the pub, then wait around and drive them home again. I was the designated driver on a learner's permit! I had to support myself, and I was having the best time doing it. I'd sit up in a cherry picker among the tops of the trees on my lunch break, looking out over the world. It was the end of my childhood – I was never a kid again. Sometimes I think when I was born, I came out as a fully grown adult. Dad said I could run before I could walk, and that's how I've always handled life.

After a while I got offered a job in the pub kitchen. The place was a bit rough, with $2 coins on the bar ready for punters to buy their next glass of beer. No frills at all! But I got into it. I started working as a dishwasher, then on to the deep-fryer. From then on, I knew I could always get a job in a pub. I had the taste for freedom and was ready to move to the next place. There were bigger fish out there for me, so I got a pack of friends together and we drove down south.

Thousands of
kilometres later,
I arrived at my new
home, Melbourne,
where my cooking
adventures really
began.

Part Two: Big City Life

Moving away from home is still one of the hardest things I've ever done. I arrived in Melbourne excited to experience the city, from the vibrant culture to the amazing food, but I had to find a job, fast. I had no idea how hard it would be for a young woman, let alone a woman of colour, to find work. This was the late nineties, and the kitchens were ruled by men. It was a challenge just to get in the door, but once I did, I was in for life. I made sure I stuck with the hospitality industry no matter how tough it got because I just loved it.

Hospitality is like a village of its own. Working long shifts in the kitchen, you end up spending most of your time with colleagues who become your family, particularly when you're far away from home and your community. We all came from somewhere else and so, for me, it was like swapping one village for another. The friends I made in kitchens and restaurants have stayed with me for life.

Outside the kitchen, it wasn't always the same story. People don't realise how big and diverse Australia really is, and I would often get asked 'Where are you from?' When I would tell them I was from the Torres Strait, I would get a blank look.

I found one of the best ways to teach people about my home was through the food I was raised with, in dishes such as yams in coconut cream (called sop sop) and semur, a chicken soy sauce dish with lots of lemongrass, ginger and vermicelli noodles.

Did you know the Torres Strait was multicultural long before the rest of Australia? Our dishes have a strong Japanese and South-East Asian influence, filtered through an Island lens. The Islands traded food, plants, baskets and nets with Papua New Guinea and Indonesia (or Makassar) for generations. The Japanese settled there as early as the mid-nineteenth century, diving for pearls and bêche-de-mer (sea cucumbers) to send back to Japan, and they married into our families and are a part of our community to this day.

Mabu Mabu

Coming from a tropical island where I would catch all my food, I had to find new ways of foraging in Melbourne. If I felt like a taste of home, I'd just go out and find it. You can forage wherever you are, whether it's in a city or on a small island. I'd find periwinkles down at Williamstown pier and use a safety pin to pop out the sea snails and eat them with rice. I would hunt through the markets and find fresh pipis for a bargain, or head to the beach and look for samphire succulents and eat like royalty.

Australia is a multicultural platform for so many different countries, and how we share culture is through food, whether it's Greek, Italian, Ethiopian, Turkish, Indian or Vietnamese. There's more acceptance through food. Great food is the key to conversation and helps open people's minds to new cultures. But, looking around Melbourne, I realised there was little understanding of Australian Indigenous food, and definitely not of Torres Strait Islander food. I knew it was time to change that.

Mabu Mabu

Part Three:
Help Yourself

Mabu Mabu means 'help yourself' in Meriam Mir. On Mer, whenever we're celebrating a special occasion such as a wedding or a tombstone opening, we pile the table high with food like damper, fried fish, scones and yams. Everyone grabs a plate and someone announces 'mabu mabu' before they all dig in. My best friend overheard me say this at my wedding a few years ago and we instantly knew it had to be the name of my business.

I started Mabu Mabu making sauces, spices and curry pastes at the South Melbourne Market. It was an idea that started between two friends – we'd been talking about it for years – and one day we saw a spot had opened up in the South Melbourne Market. We only had one day to apply! Then, once the application was in, we had less than a week to pull together our entire product line. I worked late nights in my mother-in-law's kitchen, cooking up a storm and giving my wife samples (she is the condiment queen). Getting the branding right was also really important to me. I wanted it to represent the bold flavours and colours of the Islands, so I painted the shop a bright ocean blue.

It was hard in the first year, as every dollar went straight back into the business. I started catering for friends and their families on the side, which soon took over. It was clear I needed a bigger venue. One day I saw a shopfront advertised in Yarraville. I loved the village vibe of the area, and thought it was the perfect spot for my next step – a full-time cafe! The cafe was a game-changer, and it was where I could really focus on showcasing Indigenous ingredients and flavours. I started serving versions of the food I grew up eating: damper with whipped golden syrup butter, kingfish cured with coconut and lime, and grilled emu fillet with saltbush chimichurri.

Mabu Mabu

It's not easy starting a brand from scratch – you have to commit yourself 24/7 and say 'no' in your personal life in order to have a successful business life. But Mabu Mabu is more than a business to me. I want to change people's views through serving the amazing flavours of Australia. I want to show that Blak women in business can stand up and represent. And I want to be a role model for Indigenous kids like me, who grew up on a little island or in a small community anywhere, and prove they can do anything if they work hard. It's amazing what you can achieve if you put your mind to it. I'm so proud that I can hire people – especially women of colour – to make their own way in business.

Now, just three years since starting Mabu Mabu, I'm launching my next venture, Big Esso: a 130-seat kitchen and bar at Federation Square. I would never in a hundred years have imagined that I would be opening a restaurant in Melbourne's CBD, putting Torres Strait Islander culture at the heart of this city. Who knows what I'll do next; I've got so many goals. My dad was a big dreamer, but he never got to achieve his dreams. I think I've achieved so much so quickly because I'm doing it for the both of us.

I'm on a mission to take Indigenous ingredients out of fancy restaurants and into every kitchen. Now is the time to share the amazing food culture that has been handed down to us through the generations for more than 60,000 years. Just like organic produce, native ingredients shouldn't be an expensive treat. Everyone in Australia should be cooking with native fruit, veg, spices and meats. Kara Meta, Mara Meta means 'my home, your home'. With this book, I invite you to join our village. It's time to open your heart – and your pantry – to the Torres Strait, and to the many Indigenous flavours, cuisines and cultures of this big island: Australia.

Part Four: The Native Pantry

Succulents

Aragetti (Suaeda)

This delicious succulent is prickly, like a nettle, and deeply salty, like a cross between seablite and samphire. I love using it in dips, or you can add it to risotto or pasta for colour and earthy flavour. It lasts a long time – you can have it sitting in your fridge for weeks. People are used to putting salt in everything they eat, but I like using different ingredients for seasoning. I rarely use traditional salt at Mabu Mabu and I don't put it on the table.

Karkalla

Karkalla is better known as 'pig face' and it reminds me of being at home beside the ocean. It's a sea succulent with lots of fresh crunch – like a cucumber or a cactus. There are a few different versions around, but the variety I cook with is like a beach banana, with a berry and a flower that you can eat, too. I put it on everything! It's a great addition to tacos or stir-fries, adding saltiness while grabbing all the other flavours along with it. It holds itself well in stews, and pickles amazingly.

Samphire

Eating samphire takes me right back to the Islands. When I first moved to Melbourne, I would forage for samphire down at Williamstown beach. It's quite common in coastal areas and is often known as sea asparagus. It has a salty bite and looks beautiful in dishes – almost like an insect's arm. It adds so much to a recipe, especially when you pickle it. I like combining samphire and warrigal greens to make a green sauce. You can also use samphire to give a pasta sauce vibrant colour, mix it through gnocchi, stir it in a slaw or eat it fresh.

Seablite

Seablite is my favourite! (I have a lot of favourites.) If rosemary and thyme had a baby, it would be seablite. It has soft leaves, with a deeply savoury flavour, which is perfect for quiches and tarts. The fragrance smells like sand dunes by the ocean, with a 'sea breeze' vibe.

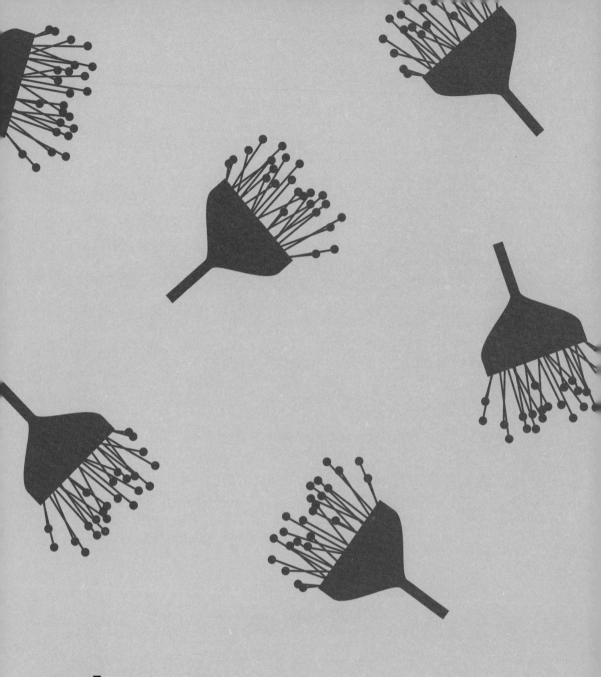

Plants
and
Herbs

Aniseed Myrtle

Aniseed myrtle reminds me of liquorice and I use it in my wattleseed hot chocolate. That little hint of aniseed is heavenly when combined with the sweetness of the chocolate and the nuttiness of wattleseed.

Cinnamon Myrtle

This is a really cool myrtle with a sweet finish. Guess what? It tastes like cinnamon, but it's sweet, as if the sugar has already been added. It is great for desserts and baking.

Crystal Ice Plant

I like adding this tasty plant to salads and tossing it through a dressing. You know when you bite into raw spinach? It tastes a bit like that, with a big rustic flavour. I like to tempura it in batter, Japanese-style, for lots of crunch.

Hibiscus

The hibiscus is a part of Island life – all the Island women like to wear it in their hair. It's got a beautiful ruby-red colour and instantly brightens up many dishes. I am a big jam girl and I love using hibiscus for jams. It has a great spicy flavour on its own and adds extra sweetness. When you grind down the flowers to make a syrup, you get translucent, almost jelly-like pieces through it. It's great in teas, cocktails and cordials, too.

Lemon Myrtle

Lemon myrtle is the queen of native herbs, and probably the most affordable. It's really a dessert herb with a citrus tang, but I also like adding it to curry pastes. You don't have to use a lot; a small pinch packs a big punch. Lemon myrtle meringues, anyone? Yes please! Or you can brew it in a tea. So delicious.

Native Thyme

Native thyme is a type of mint once used as a medicinal herb. It's pun-gent! You use native thyme as you would regular thyme, but you need to add far less as it has such a powerful flavour. There's a hint of lemon there, too, like lemon thyme. I throw it straight into my stews, tarts and sauces. It can be a hard one to find in stores, so it's the kind of thing you might need to grow yourself.

River Mint

A cousin of spearmint or peppermint, river mint is awesome when it's dry, but 100 per cent amazing when it's fresh. It reminds me of a Mintie lolly. Your mouth is like, 'What the hell just happened?' It will lift any fruity drink, especially an icy granita. It's got a concentrated punch, and people always ask, 'What is that taste?' That's the river mint.

Saltbush

There are many different types of saltbush that grow in dry or salty environments. The variety we know and love is often called 'old man saltbush', but I call it the 'Blak man's oregano'. You may have eaten saltbush lamb, which became popular when farmers would let their sheep eat the wild saltbush, which would then flavour the meat. The leaves fry up well and can look a bit like sage, with crisp grey leaves – it's really versatile and delicious.

Seaberry Saltbush

I mostly use seaberry saltbush in my cooking. It is a less salty variety with dark leaves and berries that you can blend in sauces. My saltbush chimichurri will never come off the menu at Mabu Mabu. I'm not a gravy girl (unless I'm having sausages), so I put my green sauce on everything instead. People often ask, 'When are you going to bottle your chimichurri?', but it really needs that beautiful freshness.

Sea Parsley

Sea parsley grows wild in southern coastal parts of Australia. An easy-growing plant, it can survive in pots or garden beds in part shade or full sun. The herb gives a hint of the ocean with a super refreshing zingy and peppery finish. It's great fresh in soups, or in seafood dishes.

Warrigal Greens

This is our own home-grown Australian spinach and it grows like wildfire. Why aren't we all cooking with it more? It's awesome, because it doesn't wilt away like regular spinach. I hate it when you buy a huge bag of spinach and it disappears into nothing. You should blanch your greens lightly and stir them through at the last minute so they stay firm. It's great used in pasta instead of basil, blended like an earthy pesto, and it doesn't have the metallic edge that spinach often does.

Seeds

Pepperberry

Asian cooking has the Szechuan pepper, but Australia has the pepperberry. Both have a clove-like flavour with a lingering, numbing heat. At Mabu Mabu, we don't have traditional pepper on the table; we serve pepperberry instead. It's a wet grind, not a harsh powder, and it oozes out a beautiful purple colour. I use it in stews, dips, desserts, my Christmas cake and in chai. Try adding a sprinkle to a pasta sauce – it's got such a distinct heat. It's native to Tasmania but you can find it widely. Look for it being sold under other names, such as mountain pepper.

Wattleseed

This native seed is one of my must-have staples because it's got a savoury and a sweet side. It goes well in damper, hot chocolate, waffles or pavlova, or you can use it in a massaman curry paste just as easily. It has a hazelnutty taste and a thickening, coating element that reminds me of almond meal (ground almonds). Wattleseed comes in all different colours – the darker the better. You should always roast the seeds to release the flavour. A powdered grind is best, and you can also use wattleseed like poppy seeds in baking.

Eucalyptus

Peppermint Gum

If you're looking for a pure peppermint flavour, this is where you want to start. Peppermint gum is full-on! Just a tiny pinch is like putting mouthwash in your mouth. It can almost burn your mouth with its intensity, and goes well when infused in tea, or when flavouring creams and desserts.

Strawberry Gum

You can find this in powdered form, or use the whole leaf. Think of this like a strawberry extract, but don't forget it's still a eucalyptus – it doesn't taste great without plenty of sugar. You want a subtle flavour, so don't use too much of it.

Nuts

Bunya Nut

The bunya nut is like a Brazil nut and only grows in northern Australia in the summer months. It's a great protein that works well as a snack.

Coconut

All Island dishes are coconut-based, from breakfasts to curries to curing fish. We use all of its different parts – the jelly, oil, water, milk, cream and husk. We rub it on our skin and run it through our hair. We eat it through all its different stages, from when it's young and green to hard and mature. We grate it on a madu (see page 19). We use it to make baskets, hats and bowls, and we use the leaves to wrap meats, make grass skirts and brooms. The coconut is life!

Macadamia

Everybody knows Australia's creamy, oily macadamias, and we should all be cooking with them more often. Unfortunately, it's one of the more expensive nuts out there, so make sure you use it to its full potential. Toast the nut to release the oils and it will lift everything from a salad to a stir-fry.

Sea Almonds

These are native to the Torres Strait and come from a tree called mikeer, which grows in salty environments. We crack open the fruit and feast on the nut inside, which has a subtle almond flavour and makes a delicious snack for kids. You won't be able to find this at the supermarket, but it grows in abundance in Far North Queensland.

Fruits

Bell Fruit

This Island fruit looks like beautiful pink bells hanging from the tree. I would pick them like apples and eat them fresh growing up. They're quite pale on the inside, and full of juice. I like pickling them for extra zing, like a ceviche. Bell fruit also offers crunchiness when added to cooked fish as a salsa.

Bush Tomato

You'll usually find bush tomato in dried form because they don't keep very well when fresh. They're packed with flavoursome seeds under a thin layer of skin and have a unique umami tomato flavour. I like to buy them whole-dried so I can slice them up for a powerful flavour punch. You can use bush tomato as a seasoning too; it's great in a tomato-based sauce.

Davidson Plum

Davidson plum is everywhere now, and it is known for its vibrant ruby-red colour. The flavour is quite bitter on its own, but you'll find it colouring everything from gin to sorbets.

Desert Lime

My favourite lime. Desert limes are quite small and beautiful, and become translucent when they cook down. I love making a Desert Lime Syrup (page 191) and using it in a granita or even a margarita. Desert lime is like a lime and lemon mixed together and, when used in a marmalade, it's magic.

Finger Lime

Finger limes are the caviar of the lime world, with beautiful jewels inside that burst in the mouth. It's a great garnish, but you can clean down the waxy skin, slice the fruit and eat it with the skin on for extra flavour.

Illawarra Plum

This plum isn't juicy. It is a bit smaller than a regular plum, and all the flavour comes from the skin. I love using it in a homemade barbecue sauce – it's sweet and spicy.

Many people think Kakadu plums have an anti-ageing property. They are known around the world as a superfood, and the cosmetics industry buys up most of them. Kakadu plum has loads of vitamin C. It is usually ground down into a powder and can be added to smoothies.

Kakadu Plum

Lemon Aspen

Lemon aspen has its own special tang, different to regular lemons, which gives a fresh tartness to drinks or desserts. While super tangy, it is not too full-on in flavour – I used to just grab it off the tree and eat it raw as a kid.

Everybody loves lilli pilli, especially in drinks and jams. It's not sweet on its own, but is often used for its attractive look. It's vibrant in colour, like a cherry, a currant, or even a pomegranate. You can buy your own plant and have it in the backyard.

Lilli Pilli

Muntries

Also known as emu apples, muntries are somewhere between a nashi pear and a guava. They have apple vibes, but with their own flavour. Muntries are great in a chutney, and I also love them fresh – you can eat them like candy.

Native Wild Currants

This tropical shrub grows in northern parts of Queensland. The ruby-red fruit grows in long bunches and sweetens as it matures. With the tartness and flavour of fresh cranberries and pomegranate, it's great for salads, desserts and syrups.

Quandong

Quandongs are a wild peach, but taste quite bitter until you add sugar. I use them in my famous Quandong Christmas Cake (page 198), as well as in jams, chutneys or a savoury jus. Quandong breaks down like rhubarb when you stew it. You can eat it freeze-dried or fresh. It's got medicinal qualities and the seeds can be used to make jewellery, or even flour.

Riberries

These tiny berries make beautiful jams and cordials. They have a unique flavour – spicy and clovey. Riberries can be hard to find, so get in quick if you see them.

Sorbee

I grew up climbing sorbee trees. The fruit grows on the trunk itself. It's darkish purple on the outside and white on the inside. It's similar to bell fruit. Growing up, all the oldies would cover up the tree to protect the fruit when it was in season.

Wongai

Wongai grows up north and is like an Island date. We would use the seeds to play games with. Wongai trees are rare and the fruit is only briefly in season.

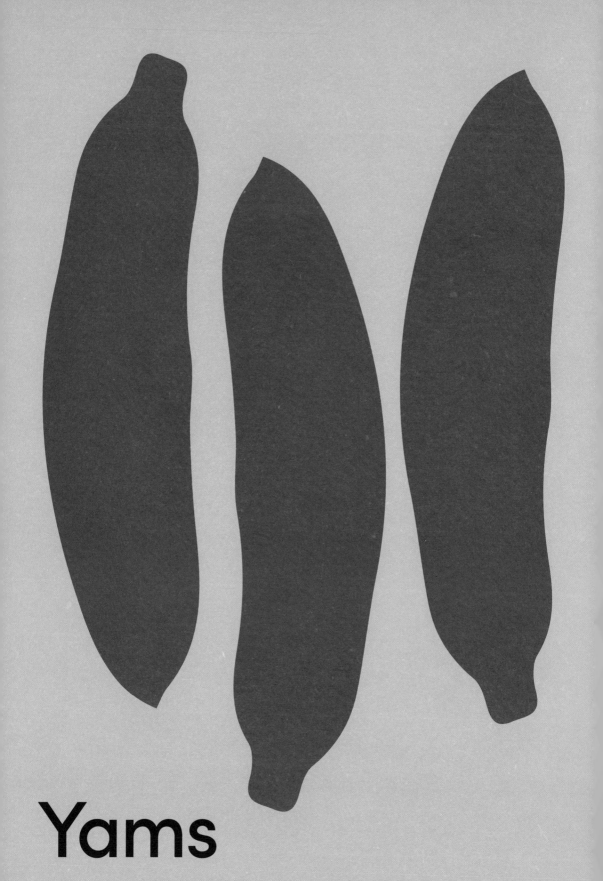

Yams

Cassava

Yams are the first thing I ever dug up as a kid. The cassava is a nutty root veg that grows like wildfire where I come from. We use it for the starch – you grate the cassava, squeeze the juice out, then let it settle. When the water clears, the starch remains underneath. You can cook cassava in coconut milk and it becomes almost like sticky rice in the celebration dish 'pakalolo' (see page 197). We also eat it like a potato: mash it, roast it in the skin – it's delicious.

This is the potato for Islanders, whether you're Māori, Fijian, from the Pacific Islands or the Torres Strait. Whether it's boiled, baked or cooked in a kup murri (underground oven), it's always on the table and goes in everything we cook. It's not starchy or floury like a potato, but it's more filling and really puts meat on your bones. One of my favourite ways to eat taro is to fry it up as chips for snacking.

Taro

White Sweet Potato

Don't be fooled, these are not sweet, but they have a sexy, bright-purple flesh inside. You'll get a beautiful colour and taste from this variety.

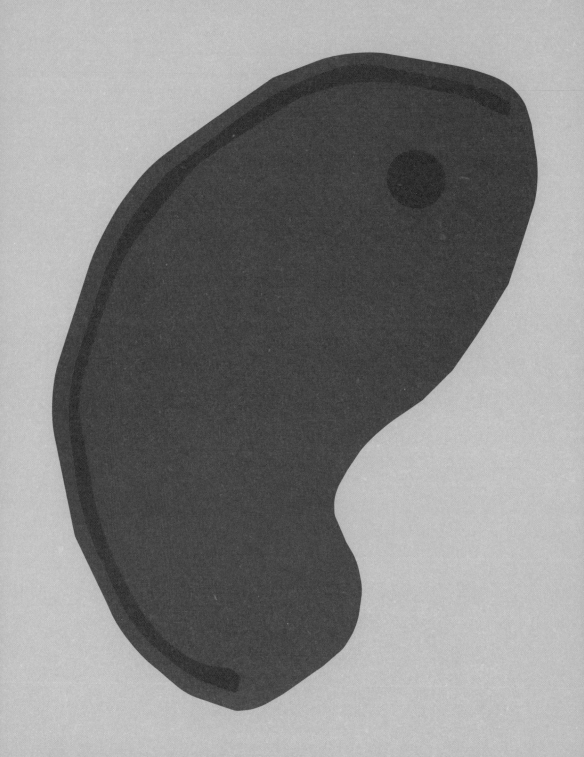

Meats

Crocodile

Crocs are like toads up north – you just have to live with them. Now you can buy crocodile fillets in the supermarket, but people often make the mistake of cooking it in thick slabs like a fish. It's actually a big, solid, muscle-bound animal, so you need to flatten the meat with a mallet to make sure it's tender. It has a reasonably bland flavour, so you'll need to give it a boost. I'm a big fan of making a pepperberry and saltbush crust and cooking croc like salt-and-pepper calamari. You can also use slices of crocodile tail, which is full of delicious marrow, or make crocodile ribs in bright green sauce.

Emu

This muscular bird has fantastic lean meat, and you want to make sure you serve it medium-rare. It has a great gamey flavour, which works really well on barbecues and grills. You want to give it some char, but not overcook it. It works like red meat, but always marinate it first. It's ideal matched with those native flavours of pepperberry and desert herbs to make it extra delicious.

Kangaroo

We all know you have to eat kangaroo on the rare side – it's great in tartare and with native thyme. We should be eating all parts of the kangaroo. My favourite is the tail, cooked bourguignon-style in red wine (see page 115). It's just like eating any kind of oxtail, where it falls off the bone after you cook it down over 6–8 hours. I'm happy to mow down an 800 g (1 lb 12 oz) beef steak. Kangaroo, on the other hand, is lean and filling, which means I eat less of it, too.

Part Five: Where to Buy Natives

These days, you can find native ingredients stocked everywhere, from the big chain supermarkets to specialty grocers and food markets. For some of the more hard-to-find ingredients used in my recipes, check out these quality Australian organic and native suppliers. You can buy ingredients online, or contact them for suggestions on where to track down items in your town or city.

Barbushco

Location New South Wales

Website barbushco.com.au

Specialty Ground lemon myrtle
Pepperberries
Saltbush
Wattleseed

Creative Native

Location Queensland

Website creativefoods.com.au

Specialty Bush tomatoes
Crocodile tails
Desert limes
Hibiscus
Muntries
Quandong
River mint
Wattleseed

Bush Lolly

Location South Australia

Website bushlolly.com

Specialty Karkalla
River mint
Fresh saltbush
Samphire
Warrigal greens

Indigiearth

Location New South Wales

Website indigiearth.com.au

Specialty Aniseed myrtle
Cinnamon myrtle
Lemon myrtle
Wattleseed

Mabu Mabu

Mabu Mabu

Location	Victoria
Website	mabumabu.com.au
Specialty	Cinnamon myrtle Hibiscus Karkalla Lemon myrtle Pepperberry Samphire Sea parsley Seablite Strawberry gum Warrigal greens Wattleseed

Snowy River Station Sea Vegetables

Location	Victoria
Website	snowyriverstation.com.au
Specialty	Karkalla Samphire Seablite Seaweeds (e.g. sea pasta, Neptune's beard) Warrigal greens

Maningrida Wild Foods

Location	Northern Territory
Website	maningridawildfoods.com
Specialty	Green ants Kakadu plums Mud crab Wild yams

Part Six: Recipes

Mabu Mabu

The oven temperatures in this book are for fan-forced ovens. If using a conventional oven, increase the temperature by 20°C (70°F).

Flour

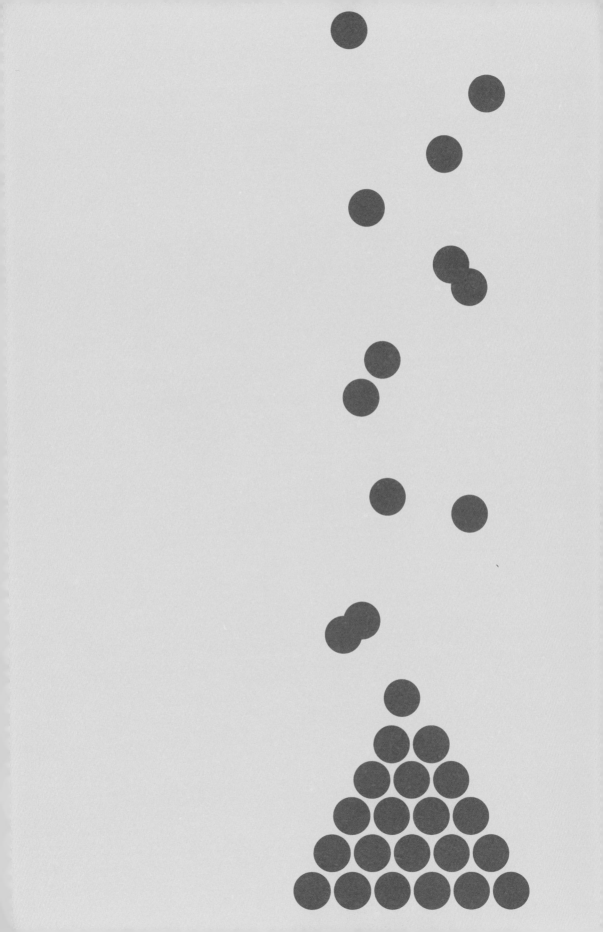

Plain Domboi

Flour is an essential part of life in the Torres Strait Islands. It's in almost every meal, and you can make so many things out of it, from savoury to sweet. Every New Year's Day, there is a flour fight. We chuck big handfuls of the stuff at each other until we're covered from head to toe, then jump in the saltwater to wash it all off. Then we start the New Year fresh. When I was living in Innisfail, I would make the drive home every other weekend to visit my cousin Joanna. She would always make me these dombois slathered with golden syrup butter for a taste of home.

Ingredients

250 g (9 oz/1⅔ cups)
   plain (all-purpose) flour,
   plus extra for dusting
Golden Syrup Butter
   (page 166), to serve

Method

1. In a bowl, mix the flour with 240 ml (8 fl oz) water to get a nice sticky dough. Flour your work surface and knead your dough until well combined.

2. Bring a pot of salted water to the boil. Cut the dough into six pieces. Roll each piece into long, finger-sized sausages. Cut each piece to finger length, then place the dough pieces in the boiling water for 3 minutes until they float to the top.

3. Once cooked, drain off the water. Eat hot with golden syrup butter.

Sabee Domboi with Fried Banana

While many kids come home from school and have a slice of bread, Island kids would always have dombois, which are similar to doughnuts and can be served savoury or sweet. They are super filling, especially when cooked 'sabee'-style in rich coconut cream. I have vivid memories of watching my aunties ripping bits of dough and throwing them into the simmering coconut cream to make this dish. It's debe lag lag (delicious)!

Method

... the pumpkin and white sweet potato in 750 ml ...ps) boiling coconut milk and 250 ml ...) water with a pinch of salt until soft.

...add the flour and 250 ml (8½ fl oz/ ...r enough to mix to a sticky dough.

...me flour onto a clean work surface and ...ugh for a few minutes, or until you have ...xtured dough (add more flour as needed ...ough from sticking to the bench and ...

...he dough to a 1 cm (½ in) thickness and ...rips about 5 cm (2 in) wide. Pull the strips ...small pieces.

...e remaining coconut milk in a large saucepan ...in the pieces of dough. Stir and allow to cook ...w minutes – the milk should be absorbed into ...ked dough.

vegetable ...

...the cooked sweet potato and pumpkin mix into ...e saucepan with the dombois and mix through.

7. For the fried banana, mix the flour, a pinch of salt and 125 ml (4 fl oz/½ cup) water into a batter in a bowl.

8. Coat the banana slices in the batter, then fry in the vegetable oil until golden. To check that your oil is hot enough, drop a pinch of flour in; if it sizzles, it's the right temperature.

9. Serve the sabee dombois with a side of fried banana.

10. For a sweeter version, drizzle over some golden syrup.

Damper

Island people make the best damper, but we do it very differently to how most Australian kids make it on their school camps. Damper is the only kind of bread I grew up with. You don't get freshly baked loaves off the barges – we just had flour and tins of butter. It was always made simply but 'Island-style': wrapped in banana leaves and steam-baked in the kup murri (underground oven). This is the first thing my dad ever taught me to cook. It's loads of fun to make and relies on simple kitchen staples. Damper also saved my business during the 2020 COVID lockdowns, when I started doing damper workshops via Zoom. These days, I'm known everywhere for my damper.

How to know when your damper is ready

I learnt to check my damper from my nan, and now my chefs at Mabu Mabu use this technique. If you grew up in a big family you might have had a relative who would tap each watermelon at the market to find the freshest, juiciest fruit for the kids. They were listening for a 'thud' to make sure the watermelon wasn't hollow. The damper technique is exactly the opposite – when you tap the bottom, your hand should bounce off the surface and you should hear a nice hollow sound. This means the damper is cooked through and ready to eat.

Makes 1 full-sized
damper, serves 4
(or 2 Island kids)

Pumpkin Damper

This is what I call the 'cheat damper'; it sneaks in a serve of vegetables without you even realising it. I'm not a great vegetable eater, but I love root vegetables. The pumpkin here gives you a vibrant natural food colouring as well. This is a huge Island favourite and I'll always remember making it with my dad.

Ingredients

500 g (1 lb 2 oz) Japanese pumpkin (squash), peeled and cubed

40 ml (1¼ fl oz) vegetable oil

450 g (1 lb/3 cups) self-raising flour, plus extra for dusting

80 g (2¾ oz) butter, at room temperature (see Notes)

1 × 50 cm (19¾ in) sheet of banana leaf (see Notes)

Golden Syrup Butter (page 166), or plain butter, to serve

Notes Banana leaves can be found fresh in many Asian markets, or frozen in Asian supermarkets.

You can use a vegan alternative to the butter here, such as Nuttelex. This works in all the damper recipes.

If you cannot source self-raising flour, you can make your own by adding 2 teaspoons baking powder to every 150 g (5½ oz/1 cup) plain (all-purpose) flour.

Method

1. Preheat the oven to 180°C (360°F).

2. Coat the pumpkin in the oil and roast in the oven until soft, almost mushy. Keep the oven on after removing the pumpkin.

3. To a bowl, add the flour and butter and mix together by rubbing between your hands until fully combined.

4. Add the cooled cooked pumpkin and mush together.

5. Add 250 ml (8½ fl oz/1 cup) water, a little at a time, and mix with your fingers until you have a nice sticky dough.

6. Place some flour on your work surface, then knead the dough until you have a bread dough consistency. Roll into a log, then set aside.

7. Before using your banana leaf, you need to release the oils to make it flexible and bring out the flavours. Hold the banana leaf over an open gas flame and move it across the flame in sections until the oils seep through the entire leaf. If you do not have a gas flame, place it in a dry non-stick frying pan for a few seconds on each side.

8. Place the dough in the centre of the banana leaf. Wrap it, folding over each end, and roll it up like a burrito. Then wrap in aluminium foil using the same method.

9. Place on the oven shelf and cook for 50–60 minutes.

10. Serve with golden syrup butter.

Saltbush and Warrigal Greens Damper

This is your dinnertime damper – and a good opportunity to throw in any green herbs you might have lying in the bottom of your crisper. Crack open the damper and eat it with hot soups, stews or anything slow-cooked to lap up all the juices. The saltbush adds an almost sourdough-like depth of flavour.

Ingredients

450 g (1 lb/3 cups) self-raising flour (see Note on page 99), plus extra for dusting

80 g (2¾ oz) butter, at room temperature (see Note on page 99), plus extra to serve

1½ tablespoons dried saltbush

100 g (3½ oz) warrigal greens, thinly sliced

1 × 50 cm (19¾ in) sheet of banana leaf (see Note on page 99)

Method

1. Preheat the oven to 180°C (360°F).

2. To a bowl, add the flour and butter and mix together using your hands until fully combined.

3. Add the saltbush and warrigal greens and mix through.

4. Add 375 ml (12½ fl oz/1½ cups) water, a little at a time, and mix with your fingers until you have a nice sticky dough.

5. Place some flour on your work surface, then knead the dough until you have a bread dough consistency. Roll into a log, then set aside.

6. Before using your banana leaf, you need to release the oils to make it flexible and bring out the flavours. Hold the banana leaf over an open gas flame and move it across the flame in sections until the oils seep through the entire leaf. If you do not have a gas flame, place it in a dry non-stick frying pan for a few seconds on each side.

7. Place the dough in the centre of the banana leaf. Wrap it, folding over each end, and roll it up like a burrito. Then wrap in aluminium foil using the same method.

8. Place on the oven shelf and cook for 50–60 minutes.

9. Serve with plain butter.

Wattleseed Damper

This is what I call the 'Blak man's coffee scroll'. The wattleseed gives the flavour of bitter chocolate, hazelnut and a hint of coffee – it's great for an afternoon snack straight from the oven with some plain butter or, even better, golden syrup butter.

Ingredients

450 g (1 lb/3 cups) self-raising flour (see Note on page 99), plus extra for dusting

80 g (2¾ oz) butter, at room temperature (see Note on page 99)

1 tablespoon ground wattleseed

Golden Syrup Butter (page 166), or plain butter, to serve

Method

1. Preheat the oven to 180°C (360°F) and dust a baking tray with flour.

2. To a bowl, add the flour and butter and mix together using your hands until fully combined.

3. Add the wattleseed and mix through.

4. Add 375 ml (12½ fl oz/1½ cups) water, a little at a time, and mix with your fingers until you have a nice sticky dough.

5. Place some flour on your work surface, then knead the dough until you have a bread dough consistency.

6. Roll into a large ball, then tuck the dough on its underside to break open the top of the loaf.

7. Place on the baking tray and bake for 40 minutes.

8. Serve with golden syrup butter.

Wattleseed Scones

When I was young, the oldies would spend the whole day yarning, and they couldn't go very long without a fresh cup of tea. It was the youngster's job to be constantly making cups of tea – and you better make it right! Even though it was just plain old black tea, it had to be made perfectly. While the adults would often eat Scotch Finger or Monte Carlo biscuits dunked in their brew, I would have been crowned best kid if I'd served some of these wattleseed scones. Yum, get in my belly! Wattleseed is great for baking and has that beautiful nutty flavour and cocoa colour that works so well in these simple scones.

Ingredients

450 g (1 lb/3 cups) self-raising flour (see Note on page 99), plus extra for dusting

100 g (3½ oz) butter, at room temperature (see Note on page 99)

375 ml (12½ fl oz/1½ cups) milk, or nut milk

1 tablespoon ground wattleseed

Strawberry Gum Cream (page 172) and Quick Lemon Myrtle Jam (page 195), to serve

Method

1. Preheat the oven to 180°C (360°F) and dust a baking tray with flour.

2. Mix the flour and butter in a bowl until well combined.

3. Add the milk and wattleseed and mix with the flour and butter to make a sticky dough.

4. Dust a clean work surface with some flour and knead the dough until it is soft in texture, being careful not to overwork it.

5. With a rolling pin, roll out the dough to a 5 cm (2 in) thickness.

6. Use a round biscuit cutter to cut out scones (if you don't have a cutter, use a measuring cup or thin glass, like a wine glass).

7. Place on the tray and bake for 20–25 minutes.

8. Serve with strawberry gum cream and lemon myrtle jam.

Wattleseed Banana Bread

Banana trees are always growing in our backyards up north, so the banana is a big staple. This is a great way to use up all your ripe bananas, and the delicious cinnamon myrtle and pepperberry show how easy it is to use native produce in your everyday cooking.

Ingredients

140 g (5 oz) brown sugar

250 g (9 oz/1⅔ cups) plain (all-purpose) flour

2 teaspoons ground cinnamon

½ teaspoon ground cinnamon myrtle

½ teaspoon ground or freshly grated nutmeg

½ teaspoon ground pepperberry

1 tablespoon ground wattleseed

150 g (5½ oz) whole macadamia nuts

5 ripe bananas

2 large eggs

125 g (4½ oz/½ cup) butter, melted and cooled, plus extra for greasing

1 tablespoon vanilla extract

125 ml (4 fl oz/½ cup) vegetable oil

Method

1. Preheat the oven to 180°C (360°F).

2. Lightly grease an 11 × 21 cm (4¼ × 8¼ in) loaf (bar) tin, and line the base and two sides with baking paper.

3. Sift all the dry ingredients into a bowl and add the macadamia nuts.

4. In a separate bowl, mash four of the bananas and mix in the eggs, butter, vanilla extract and oil.

5. Fold the dry ingredients into the wet mix until well combined.

6. Spoon the mixture into the prepared loaf tin. Slice the fifth banana and place the slices on top of the mixture.

7. Bake for 50–60 minutes.

8. To check if the bread is cooked, insert a cake skewer in the centre – the skewer should come out clean.

9. Let the bread sit in the tin for 5 minutes, then turn it out onto a wire rack.

Island to Mainland

Semur Chicken

Semur chicken and its sidekick, Sop Sop (page 112), always feature on the menu at Mabu Mabu. Semur is a hearty staple dish where a whole chicken is cooked in a thick soy broth with vermicelli noodles. The Asian flavours of lemongrass, soy and chilli feature in many Torres Strait Island dishes, influenced by the multiculturalism in the Straits that existed long before it did in the rest of Australia. Japanese fishers and divers have been living on the Islands since the nineteenth century, attracted by the bêche-de-mer (sea cucumber) and pearling industries. Torres Strait Islanders incorporated these Asian flavours into their cooking, along with ingredients from even older visitors from the surrounding islands of Papua New Guinea and Indonesia. In this Mabu Mabu version of Semur chicken, I've enhanced the recipe by adding new flavours and techniques, and some fantastic native vegetables from all over Australia. It tastes even better the next day.

Ingredients

1 whole chicken
60 ml (2 fl oz/¼ cup) vegetable oil, preferably macadamia oil
1 onion, sliced
5 garlic cloves, minced
10 cm (4 in) piece fresh ginger, peeled and finely sliced
2 lemongrass stalks, crushed and chopped into 5 cm (2 in) pieces
1 tablespoon chilli paste
250 ml (8½ fl oz/1 cup) soy sauce
750 ml (25½ fl oz/3 cups) dark beer (preferably Guinness), or replace with vegetable stock
½ teaspoon whole pepperberries
250 g (9 oz) vermicelli noodles
handful of karkalla (see Note)
handful of warrigal greens (see Note)
120 g (4½ oz/1 cup) chopped spring onion (scallion)
cooked rice, to serve

Note If you can't find karkalla and warrigal greens, replace with other green vegetables, such as bok choy or silverbeet (Swiss chard).

Method

1. Chop the chicken into large, chunky pieces (leave on the bone).

2. Heat the oil in a large pot over a high heat and brown the chicken.

3. Add the onion, garlic, ginger, lemongrass and chilli paste, and cook until the onion is browned.

4. Add the soy sauce and cook for 10–15 minutes.

5. Add the beer and pepperberries, then slow-cook, covered, over a medium heat for at least 30 minutes, or until the chicken is cooked through and just falling off the bone.

6. Once the chicken is cooked, in a separate bowl, place the vermicelli in hot water until clear, then drain and add to the pot.

7. Add the karkalla, warrigal greens and spring onion and cook for a further 10 minutes.

8. Serve with rice in bowls.

Sop Sop

Sop sop is a rich yam dish slow-cooked in coconut milk. The sweet coconut and yam flavours always remind me of home, of celebrations, and of family. If you ever brought a partner home to meet the family, an aunty would ask if you'd made sop sop for them yet – if not, they're obviously not a keeper! It's said that if you make this dish for your loved one, they will always stay with you.

Ingredients

500 g (1 lb 2 oz) peeled cassava
500 g (1 lb 2 oz) white sweet potato
500 g (1 lb 2 oz) peeled Japanese pumpkin (squash)
500 g (1 lb 2 oz) taro
1 onion
500 ml (17 fl oz/2 cups) coconut cream
1 litre (34 fl oz/4 cups) coconut milk
250 ml (8½ fl oz/1 cup) vegetable stock
2 tablespoons celery salt
cooked rice, to serve

Method

1. Cut the cassava, sweet potato, pumpkin and taro into chunky cubes and dice the onion. Place in a large saucepan.

2. Add the coconut cream and milk, stock and celery salt.

3. Simmer gently over a low heat until the vegetables have cooked through, broken down and fallen apart in the mixture.

4. Serve with cooked rice.

Kangaroo Tail Bourguignon

You don't often find a kangaroo tail in the meat aisle at the supermarket, but Aboriginal people have been eating it for generations. They know it has some of the juiciest meat, and sometimes the best bits come from what other people don't want. Whenever we cook an animal on the Islands, we make sure we eat the whole thing – waste not, want not – and so at Mabu Mabu, we make this bourguignon with the tail, too.

Ingredients

2 kg (4 lb 6 oz) kangaroo tail pieces

40 ml (1¼ fl oz) vegetable oil, plus extra for coating the pumpkin

2 garlic cloves, peeled

1 thyme sprig

1 teaspoon saltbush

1 tablespoon ground pepperberry

750 ml (25½ fl oz/3 cups) rich red wine (the heavier the better)

100 g (3½ oz) tomato paste (concentrated purée)

500 ml (17 fl oz/2 cups) tomato passata (puréed tomatoes)

1 teaspoon salt

1 teaspoon whole pepperberries

1 litre (34 fl oz/4 cups) vegetable stock

1 kg (2 lb 3 oz) Japanese pumpkin (squash), cut into wedges

3 large silverbeet (Swiss chard) leaves, sliced

karkalla, to garnish

Method

1. Start by sealing your kangaroo tail in a hot pan to give each piece a little bit of colour.

2. Add the sealed kangaroo to a nice heavy pot with the oil, then add the garlic, thyme, saltbush and ground pepperberry. Cook for 5 minutes over a medium heat.

3. Add the red wine and cook for 2 minutes, then add the tomato paste, passata, salt, whole pepperberries and stock. Cover the pot and cook over a medium–low heat for 4 hours until the meat is falling off the bone.

4. Preheat the oven to 180°C (360°F). Coat the pumpkin wedges in oil and roast for 40 minutes until soft and golden.

5. About 15 minutes before turning off the kangaroo, add the silverbeet to the top, without mixing it in, cover the pot and steam until tender.

6. Serve the kangaroo bourguignon with the silverbeet and a side of roast pumpkin wedges, garnished with karkalla.

Kangaroo Tartare

This dish is so beautiful and gamey, but also quite light. Pepperberry is a match made in heaven for kangaroo, which is delicious raw. This recipe takes a few cues from European cooking and elevates the kangaroo to the next level.

Ingredients

300 g (10½ oz) kangaroo fillet, finely chopped
1 teaspoon chopped capers
1 tablespoon snipped chives
4 sea parsley sprigs, chopped
½ teaspoon ground pepperberry
2 shallots, finely diced
½ teaspoon English mustard
2 tablespoons labne
1 tablespoon Worcestershire sauce
taro crisps, to serve

Method

1. Toss the kangaroo, capers, chives, parsley, pepperberry and shallots together in a bowl.

2. In another bowl, combine the mustard, labne and Worcestershire sauce.

3. Serve the kangaroo with a side of the labne mixture and taro crisps.

Saltbush Pepperberry Crocodile

Crocodile can be tough so you should tenderise your fillet with a mallet before you cook it – it's similar to calamari in that it hardens quickly. You'll most likely buy the tail fillet, but I prefer cooking with 'croc chops' (with the bone in), as the marrow adds more flavour.

Ingredients

150 g (5½ oz/1 cup) plain
  (all-purpose) flour
1 teaspoon ground
  pepperberry
1 teaspoon dried saltbush
1 tablespoon paprika
1 tablespoon onion powder
400 g (14 oz) crocodile tail
  meat, thinly sliced
500 ml (17 fl oz/2 cups)
  vegetable oil, for frying
Spicy Desert Lime and
  Watermelon Salad
  (page 133), to serve
chilli mayonnaise, to serve
karkalla, to garnish (optional)

Marinade
500 ml (17 fl oz/2 cups)
  buttermilk
½ teaspoon paprika
½ teaspoon dried saltbush

Method

1. Place the flour and spices in a bowl and mix well.

2. Combine the marinade ingredients in a large bowl and marinate the crocodile meat in the mixture for 20 minutes.

3. Drain off any excess marinade, then coat the crocodile meat with the spiced flour.

4. Heat the oil to 180°C (360°F) in a heavy-based pot and fry the crocodile for 5 minutes until crispy on the outside.

5. Serve with my spicy watermelon salad and chilli mayonnaise and garnish with karkalla if you like.

Sabee Curry Chicken

Sabee means 'cooked in coconut'. You'll see variations on chicken curry in many international cuisines, from India to Thailand. This is our version of the classic, and it's made at every big do. The first time I made this recipe for my cousins, they judged me, hard! Because I'm a chef, their standards for my cooking are high. I find it's best to keep it simple, and this delicious coconut curry recipe never fails.

Ingredients

1 whole chicken
2 tablespoons macadamia oil
2 garlic cloves, crushed
10 cm (4 in) piece fresh
   ginger, sliced
1 onion, diced
2 tablespoons Curry Powder
   (page 173)
10 g (¼ oz) salt
5 g (⅛ oz) ground pepper
1 litre (34 fl oz/4 cups)
   coconut milk
300 g (10½ oz) snake (yard-
   long) beans, cut into bite-
   sized pieces
cooked rice, to serve
lime wedges, to serve

Method

1. The Island way is to cut up the chicken into big chunks with the bone in.

2. Heat the macadamia oil over a high heat in a saucepan and brown the garlic, ginger and onion.

3. Add the curry powder and stir until blended.

4. Place the chicken in the pot with the spices, add the salt and pepper and continue stirring for a few minutes until the juice is released from the meat.

5. Add about 400 ml (13½ fl oz) water, cover and let steam for about 20 minutes, adding more water if necessary.

6. Next, add half the coconut milk and simmer gently over a medium heat for about 25 minutes. From time to time, stir the meat and add more coconut milk as it evaporates.

7. Add the snake beans and continue simmering until the meat is tender and the gravy is rich.

8. Serve on top of cooked rice, with lime on the side.

Pawpaw Island Curry

Kangaroo and pawpaw join together brilliantly here. Pawpaw is a very common tropical fruit that we use fresh and in all sorts of dishes. The lean kangaroo makes a lighter sort of curry – it's a real mix of sweet and savoury. Salty karkalla, sweet pawpaw, spicy curry paste: it all works. You could serve this in a lettuce cup for a summer bite.

Ingredients

1 green pawpaw (about 1 kg/2 lb 3 oz)

80 ml (2½ fl oz/⅓ cup) macadamia oil

1 teaspoon Curry Paste (page 173)

250 g (9 oz) minced (ground) kangaroo steak

5 cm (2 in) piece fresh ginger, grated

2 bacon rashers (slices), diced

1 teaspoon sugar

1 tablespoon sultanas (golden raisins)

100 g (3½ oz) karkalla

cooked rice or lettuce cups, to serve

Method

1. Peel the pawpaw, discard the seeds and cut the fruit into cubes.

2. Heat the oil in a frying pan and add the curry paste.

3. Add the pawpaw, kangaroo, ginger and bacon and stir over a good heat for about 5 minutes.

4. Turn down the heat and add the sugar, 250 ml (8½ fl oz/1 cup) water and the sultanas.

5. Simmer until the pawpaw is cooked, about 30 minutes, taking care not to overcook it.

6. Toss the karkalla through at the end.

7. Serve with rice or in lettuce cups.

Wild Boar in Dinagwan

This is a true hunter's dish, and I will admit: it is not for the faint-hearted. Dinagwan means 'to cook the animal in its own blood'. Growing up, my dad would go out hunting with the dogs to find a boar to eat for special occasions. He'd drain off the blood and then use it to stew the meat. We're normally fish eaters or yam eaters, but this is a celebration dish. We make sure we use all the parts of the pig – ask your local butcher to source pig's blood if you want to give this a try.

Ingredients

1 litre (34 fl oz/4 cups) pig's blood
400 ml (13½ fl oz) white vinegar
110 g (4 oz) salt
80 ml (2½ fl oz/⅓ cup) vegetable oil
80 g (2¾ oz) piece fresh ginger, peeled and grated
4 garlic cloves, minced
5 kg (11 lb) boar belly, or pork belly, cut into 2 cm (¾ in) cubes
1 tablespoon native thyme
bunch of native tea grass, or lemongrass
cooked rice, to serve
pasta seaweed, to garnish (optional)

Lemon Myrtle Yoghurt
200 g (7 oz) plain yoghurt
½ teaspoon ground lemon myrtle
10 ml (¼ fl oz) lemon juice
pinch of ground white pepper

Method

1. Blend the blood, vinegar and salt and set aside to congeal.

2. Heat the oil in a large pan over a high heat and brown the ginger and the garlic. Add the boar belly, congealed blood, native thyme and tea grass, reduce the heat and simmer for about 45 minutes until the meat is cooked.

3. When cooked, the pork will be coated in a rich gravy and the sauce should not be runny.

4. Combine the lemon myrtle yoghurt ingredients in a bowl and stir.

5. Serve with rice and yoghurt and garnish with seaweed, if using.

Tin Meat and Rice

This is my dad's favourite recipe. When money was tight, we lived in one bedroom and shared the kitchen with four other adults. My first taste of beef came from a tin of corned beef – it's a staple for every Island kitchen. My dad used to make it five different ways, including with raw onions in a sandwich, in a curry paste, or in a broth.

Ingredients

1 onion, finely diced
1 tablespoon vegetable oil
1 tin corned beef
1 tablespoon Keen's curry powder
2 spring onions (scallions), sliced
cooked rice, to serve

Method

1. Fry the onion in the hot oil until golden brown, then add the corned beef, break it up and cook for 10 minutes.

2. Add the curry powder and spring onion and fry for 5 minutes, then remove the pan from the heat.

3. Curried tin meat is always served with steamed rice.

Pulled Wild Boar

Wild boar is available from any specialty butcher – it is gamier in flavour and doesn't have as much fat as the more common pork neck. The recipe is sweetened by the apple juice and makes a more natural, leaner version of traditional pulled pork. Pile it into a fresh brioche roll with some chunks of cos (romaine) lettuce for crunch.

Ingredients

2 boar necks
60 ml (2 fl oz/¼ cup) vegetable oil
230 g (8 oz/1 cup, firmly packed) brown sugar
2 tablespoons onion powder
2 tablespoons garlic powder
2 tablespoons paprika
1 tablespoon ground pepperberry
2 tablespoons salt
1 litre (34 fl oz/4 cups) apple juice
500 ml (17 fl oz/2 cups) vegetable stock
brioche buns and cos (romaine) lettuce, to serve

Method

1. Rub the boar necks with the oil, brown sugar, onion powder, garlic powder, paprika, pepperberry and salt.

2. Place your necks, apple juice and veggie stock in a large pot and slow-cook over a medium heat, stirring regularly, for 1½ hours until the meat is fully broken down – then it's ready to eat.

3. Serve in a fresh brioche bun with cos lettuce chunks.

Wattleseed Spatchcock

This is smarter than your average fried chicken. You could use regular chook, but make sure you cook it on the bone, which keeps the bird extra juicy. The wattleseed and saltbush make a delicious crisp coating – I call it 'the Blak lady crumb'.

Ingredients

150 g (5½ oz/1 cup) plain (all-purpose) flour
1 tablespoon paprika
1 tablespoon dried saltbush
1 tablespoon garlic powder
1 tablespoon onion powder
40 g (1½ oz) finely ground wattleseed
2 tablespoons salt
2 whole butterflied spatchcocks
2 litres (68 fl oz/8 cups) vegetable oil
sliced watermelon, to serve
karkalla, to garnish
fried saltbush, to garnish (optional)
native currants, to garnish (optional)

Marinade
1 litre (34 fl oz/4 cups) buttermilk
1 tablespoon paprika
1 tablespoon dried saltbush

Method

1. Mix the flour, paprika, saltbush, the garlic and onion powders, wattleseed and salt together on a plate and set aside.

2. Chop the spatchcocks into pieces, cutting at the joints, thighs and the wings.

3. Mix the marinade ingredients in a bowl and let your spatchcock pieces marinate for 20 minutes.

4. Heat the oil to 160°C (320°F) in a heavy-based pot. To check that your oil is hot enough, drop a pinch of flour in; if it sizzles immediately, it's the right temperature.

5. Coat your spatchcock pieces well in the flour mixture, place in the hot oil, reduce the temperature so the oil simmers and fry each piece for 8 minutes until tender.

6. Serve with watermelon, garnished with karkalla, saltbush and native currants, if using.

Barbecue Emu

This molasses marinade is delicious; the sweet syrup gives you great char as soon as the meat hits the hotplate. Emu should be served medium-rare and still pink; it's a red meat and should never be overcooked.

Ingredients

80 ml (2½ fl oz/⅓ cup) olive oil
2 tablespoons brown sugar
2 tablespoons Dijon mustard
½ teaspoon ground
  pepperberry
1 tablespoon sea salt
80 g (2¾ oz) molasses
1 kg (2 lb 3 oz) emu flat fillet

**Saltbush and Warrigal
  Greens Chimichurri**
1 bunch parsley
2 bunches coriander
  (cilantro)
4 shallots, peeled
5 garlic cloves, peeled
1 tablespoon dried saltbush
100 g (3½ oz) fresh saltbush
300 g (10½ oz) warrigal
  greens
250 ml (8½ fl oz/1 cup)
  vegetable oil
1 teaspoon sea salt
2 long red chillies
150 ml (5 fl oz) red-wine
  vinegar

Method

1. Mix together the oil, sugar, mustard, pepperberry, salt and molasses in a bowl.

2. Add the emu fillet and marinate for 2 hours.

3. Heat a barbecue to high and grill the emu fillet on each side for 5 minutes.

4. Let the meat rest for 10 minutes.

5. While the meat is resting, blend all chimichurri ingredients until chunky (don't overprocess!).

6. Slice the emu and serve with chimichurri.

Spicy Desert Lime and Watermelon Salad

This sweet-savoury salad is power-packed with flavour. The sweetness of the watermelon – one of my favourite fruits – combines with the sharpness of desert lime and the creamy goat's cheese. This is a great use for Pickled Succulents (page 175), which are a tangy, salty flavour bomb.

Ingredients

1 kg (2 lb 3 oz) watermelon, cut into pieces

125 ml (4 fl oz/½ cup) olive oil

100 ml (3½ fl oz) red-wine vinegar

80 g (2¾ oz/½ cup) seablite leaves

5 g (⅛ oz) sea salt

80 g (2¾ oz) whole desert limes, sliced

80 ml (2½ fl oz/⅓ cup) lime juice

1 tablespoon native currants

2 shallots, thinly sliced

100 g (3½ oz) Pickled Succulents (page 175)

80 g (2¾ oz) crumbled goat's cheese

80 g (2¾ oz/½ cup) caperberries, sliced

1 spring onion (scallion), sliced

10 g (¼ oz/½ cup) sea parsley leaves

Method

1. Place the watermelon pieces, olive oil, vinegar, seablite, sea salt, desert limes, lime juice and native currants in a bowl and leave to marinate for 20 minutes.

2. Toss through the rest of the ingredients and eat immediately.

Poached Spicy Mushrooms

I taught myself how to make this dish after eating something similar at a deli in London. It riffs on the idea of poaching a variety of mushrooms and then cooking them in herbs and spices. You really honour all the flavours of the mushroom and elevate them with the second cooking process. It's a dish that keeps on giving.

Ingredients

500 ml (17 fl oz/2 cups) red-wine vinegar
5 bay leaves
3 garlic cloves, sliced
½ teaspoon whole pepperberries
100 g (3½ oz) enoki mushrooms
200 g (7 oz) oyster mushrooms, sliced
200 g (7 oz) shiitake mushrooms
200 g (7 oz) king brown mushrooms, sliced
1 tablespoon vegetable oil
1 tablespoon native thyme
1 tablespoon chilli paste
100 g (3½ oz) samphire
100 g (3½ oz) karkalla
lettuce cups, to serve

Method

1. In a large pot, combine 1 litre (34 fl oz/4 cups) water, the vinegar, bay leaves, half the garlic and the pepperberries and boil for 30 minutes. Add the mushrooms and poach for 10 minutes, then drain and strain off the liquid. Set the mushrooms aside.

2. In a large frying pan, heat the oil and fry the remaining garlic, the mushrooms, thyme, chilli paste, samphire and karkalla for 5 minutes before adding salt to taste.

3. Eat with lettuce cups.

Hot Seaweed Eggs

This is a dish I designed just for me that appears on the Mabu Mabu Tuckshop menu. I eat it very regularly. In almost every cafe, you'll find a chilli scramble, but it often isn't spicy or very interesting. People get blown away by how spicy this version is. I even created my own chilli paste just to go in this dish, which now sits on all the tables in the cafe. The seaweed is also a winner here – pasta seaweed looks like a ribbon, and bearded seaweed looks exactly like a beard! You can find dried versions at Asian grocers, or buy them fresh from specialty suppliers. The trick to a great scrambled egg is to make sure you cook it on a nice high heat to start, so you don't overcook your egg.

Ingredients

5 eggs
10 ml (¼ fl oz) vegetable oil
60 g (2 oz/¼ cup) karkalla
1 spring onion (scallion), finely sliced
30 g (1 oz/½ cup) pasta seaweed
30 g (1 oz/½ cup) bearded seaweed
1 teaspoon My Favourite Chilli Paste (page 176)
1 tablespoon fried shallots
toast, to serve

Method

1. Whisk your eggs well.

2. To a nice hot pan, add the oil, karkalla, spring onion and the pasta seaweed and cook for 1 minute.

3. Add the eggs, bearded seaweed, chilli paste and shallots, reduce the heat and make sure to fold your eggs for 40 seconds.

4. Take off the heat and serve up on some crispy toast.

Ocean

Breakfast of Champions

Oysters are my all-time favourite thing to eat for a seafood breakfast, because it reminds me so much of home. It's a real Island breakfast: fresh, plump, creamy oysters boosted with a salty hit of karkalla and a tangy dressing. I don't drink coffee, so this is how I start my day.

Ingredients

12 fresh karkalla sprigs
1 finger lime
12 oysters (preferably St Helens), shucked

Mignonette Dressing
100 ml (3½ fl oz) white-wine vinegar
100 ml (3½ fl oz) red-wine vinegar
½ teaspoon crushed pepperberry
½ teaspoon lemon aspen powder
½ teaspoon salt
50 g (1¾ oz) caster (superfine) sugar
2 shallots, finely sliced

Method

1. For the dressing, mix all of the ingredients in a small bowl until the sugar has dissolved.

2. Garnish the freshly shucked oysters with karkalla and finger lime caviar and add a dash of mignonette dressing.

Serves 4

Namas

This dish is prepared in a similar style to ceviche. It's always best to make it with fresh fish straight out of the ocean. The raw fish will cure in the citrus and coconut to create a smooth, fragrant and refreshing starter that is perfect on a warm spring or summer day. The hint of soy brings these multicultural flavours together.

Ingredients

800 g (1 lb 12 oz) kingfish, skin removed
1 long red chilli, finely diced
¼ bunch of coriander (cilantro), thinly sliced
100 ml (3½ fl oz) freshly squeezed lime juice
250 ml (8½ fl oz/1 cup) thick coconut cream (I use Kara brand)
2 tablespoons dark soy sauce
pinch of sea salt
taro chips, to serve

Method

1. Slice the kingfish into thin sashimi slices and add to a bowl with the chilli, coriander and lime juice. Set aside for 10 minutes

2. Add the coconut cream, soy sauce and a pinch of sea salt, then mix together.

3. Marinate in the refrigerator for 15 minutes before serving. Serve with taro chips.

Fried Sardines

When you grow up with nothing, you'll always find a way to put food on the table. I would often go down to the wharf on Horn Island with a hand reel and the biggest hook I could find, then lower the line down into a school of small sardines. Then I'd give the line a hard jig and hook up the sardines. I'd catch enough for dinner and head home to roast them up – yum.

I love sardines cooked on an open flame to give you a nice char. Cooking them straight on the barbecue is the best way to replicate the same crispness.

Ingredients

500 g (1 lb 2 oz) sardines
olive oil, for rubbing
pinch of dried saltbush
handful of chopped sea
  parsley
pinch of sea salt
lemon juice, to serve

Method

1. In a bowl, give your sardines a good rub with some oil, the saltbush, sea parsley and a pinch of sea salt.

2. Heat a barbecue to high and cook the sardines on each side for 2–3 minutes.

3. Serve up with a good splash of lemon juice.

Lemon Aspen Mussels

This recipe reminds me of foraging for fresh seafood – it's such an easy recipe to throw together quickly for a delicious meal. The mussels open up in just a few minutes in the peppery broth, and the lemon aspen gives a great zesty flavour without using lemons. You could also use periwinkles if you can find them at the market.

Ingredients

1 kg (2 lb 3 oz) mussels
4 shallots, sliced
4 native thyme sprigs
1 tablespoon olive oil
5 g (⅛ oz) pepperberry leaf
3 tablespoons tomato paste
  (concentrated purée)
1 teaspoon chilli paste
½ teaspoon ground
  pepperberry
1 teaspoon lemon aspen
  powder
pinch of sea salt
200 ml (7 fl oz) white wine
handful of chopped sea
  parsley
3 tablespoons karkalla
Saltbush and Warrigal
  Greens Damper (page 102),
  to serve

Method

1. Make sure to clean your mussels before cooking. You will see a little hairy bit sticking out from the side – this is called the beard, and all you need to do is pull it downwards towards the smaller end of the mussel to remove it, and they're ready to use.

2. In a large, heavy frying pan with a lid, cook your shallots and thyme in the olive oil with the pepperberry leaf for 3 minutes over a high heat until the shallots are tender. Add the mussels and tomato paste and place the lid on to steam for 3 minutes.

3. Just as the mussels start to open, add your chilli paste, ground pepperberry, lemon aspen, a pinch of sea salt and the wine, then close the lid and cook for another 3 minutes. Your mussels should be fully opened.

4. Toss through the sea parsley and karkalla and serve with some slices of saltbush damper.

Ginger Periwinkles in Broth

Periwinkles, or sea snails, are the ultimate shellfish. These are almost like escargot – salty and slightly chewy, in a good way. Back in the day, I used to forage periwinkles down at Williamstown and pull them from their shells with a pin. This recipe uses a spicy broth that makes the seafood shine, using lots of zesty lemongrass and ginger.

Ingredients

2 kg (4 lb 6 oz) periwinkles
2 lemongrass stalks, sliced
2 long red chillies, roughly sliced
10 cm (4 in) piece fresh ginger, sliced
5 garlic cloves, peeled
2 shallots, sliced
½ teaspoon whole pepperberries
1 tablespoon olive oil
2 litres (68 fl oz/8 cups) fish stock
5 whole pepperberry leaves
2 spring onions (scallions) roughly sliced
125 g (4½ oz/½ cup) chilli aioli, to serve

Method

1. Wash and soak the periwinkles in cold water for an hour. Repeat three times.

2. In a large pot, fry the lemongrass, chilli, ginger, garlic, shallots, pepperberries and periwinkles in the oil over a high heat for 10 minutes.

3. Add the fish stock, pepperberry leaves and spring onion and boil for 30 minutes.

4. To eat, use a skewer or needle to pick out the meat from the periwinkles and dip in some chilli aioli.

Blue Swimmer Crab with Red Pepper Sauce

When I was in my late twenties, I discovered I was allergic to a lot of foods, such as milk and tomatoes. I developed this recipe because I really missed eating Italian-style red sauce, and it uses capsicums (bell peppers) instead of tomatoes. I've also included this recipe because it's my wife's favourite, and one of the first things I ever cooked for her.

Ingredients

3 blue swimmer crabs
6 red capsicums (bell peppers)
4 garlic cloves, crushed
2 tablespoons chilli paste
1 teaspoon whole pepperberries
2 tablespoons tomato paste (concentrated purée)
40 ml (1¼ fl oz) vegetable oil
500 ml (17 fl oz/2 cups) fish stock
1 tablespoon dried saltbush
5 spring onions (scallions), sliced roughly
handful of sea parsley, chopped
Saltbush and Warrigal Greens Damper (page 102), to serve

Method

1. Clean the crabs – open your crab from the bottom, pry open its head to find and remove the filters.

2. Bring a large pot of salted water to the boil.

3. Place the crabs in the boiling water for 4 minutes, then move them to a bowl of ice to cool.

4. Roast the capsicums whole in the oven at 180°C (360°F) for 30–35 minutes, then peel off the skin and discard the seeds. Purée the capsicums in a blender.

5. In a large pan or wok, fry the garlic, chilli, pepperberries and tomato paste in the vegetable oil over a medium heat for 7 minutes, then add the puréed capsicums, fish stock and saltbush.

6. Add the crabs to the sauce, cook for 3 minutes, then add the spring onion and sea parsley and cook for another 3 minutes.

7. Serve with saltbush damper.

Butterflied Garfish (Zabeere)

Zabeere, or garfish, is every aunty's favourite fish, because they will usually catch more of these than the men out on the water hunting the big fish! The first time you go fishing with your aunty as a kid, she'll give you a small hand reel fishing line with a tiny hook, and a small ball of dough for bait. You might think she doesn't want you to waste the good bait, but look over and you'll see she has an even bigger ball of dough on her hook. Aunty throws the line into the ocean and your hooks float on the top of the water. Little do you know, zabeere love to swim on the surface, so before you know it – bam – you've made your first catch.

Ingredients

4 whole garfish (deboned
    and butterflied; ask your
    fishmonger to do this for you)
plain (all-purpose) flour,
    for dusting
pinch of ground pepperberry
lemon aspen salt, to taste
1 tablespoon olive oil
cooked rice, to serve

Method

1. Lightly dust the garfish with flour, pepperberry and some lemon aspen salt.

2. Add the oil to a pan and fry the garfish over a medium heat until nicely golden – it'll only take around 3 minutes for each side.

3. Serve with rice.

Samphire Razor Clams

Samphire, the salty sea cucumber, goes so well with these clams.
Here, you're cooking the clams in their own juices with a spicy chilli finish.
Any fishmonger should have razor clams – it's a larger style of clam than
the more common pipi.

Ingredients

1 onion, diced
1 garlic clove, crushed
100 g (3½ oz) samphire
2 bacon rashers (slices),
  chopped
2 tablespoons vegetable oil
2 kg (4 lb 6 oz) razor clams
2 teaspoons plain
  (all-purpose) flour
60 ml (2 fl oz/¼ cup) vinegar
1 teaspoon lemon juice
1 teaspoon prawn paste
2 bird's eye chillies, crushed
1 teaspoon salt
finely chopped shallots,
  to garnish

Method

1. In a large pan, fry the onion, garlic, samphire
and bacon in the oil over a high heat until browned.
Add the clams.

2. Make a paste with the flour, vinegar, lemon juice,
prawn paste and chillies.

3. Add enough water to make 250 ml (8½ fl oz/1 cup)
of liquid and add it to the frying pan.

4. Reduce the heat to medium. Simmer for 30 minutes,
adding more water as the sauce evaporates, until you
are left with a dark sauce. Season with the salt and
garnish with finely chopped shallots.

Stuffed Squid

I'm a real rice girl and I love squid, so this is one of my favourite dishes. I grew up catching squid on the rocks every morning, and this is how I wish I could have cooked it back then. It's a Spanish-style recipe with a native spin – buy some good-quality morcilla (blood sausage) and it will add loads of richness and flavour.

Ingredients

2 morcilla sausages, diced
1 chorizo sausage, diced
370 g (13 oz/2 cups) cooked
   arborio rice
2 spring onions (scallions),
   thinly sliced
1 tablespoon sea salt
1 teaspoon paprika
¼ teaspoon ground
   pepperberry
10 g (¼ oz/½ cup) sea
   parsley, chopped
leaves from 3 seablite sprigs
80 ml (2½ fl oz/⅓ cup) lemon
   juice
½ tablespoon vegetable oil
4 medium-sized squid tubes
2 litres (68 fl oz/8 cups)
   vegetable stock
chilli aioli, to serve

Method

1. Fry the sausages, rice, spring onion, salt, paprika, pepperberry, sea parsley, seablite and lemon juice in the oil in a large pan over a medium heat until well combined. Set aside to cool for 5 minutes.

2. Stuff the rice mix into the squid tubes, then tightly wrap in heatproof plastic wrap.

3. Heat the vegetable stock in a saucepan to a rolling boil, then reduce to a gentle simmer and poach the squid tubes for 10 minutes.

4. Unwrap the squid tubes and place on a hot barbecue for 3 minutes each side to get a nice char on them.

5. Slice into finger-width pieces and serve with chilli aioli.

Ginger Chilli Pipis

I love this dish, as the chilli brings out the power of the pipis. Many people don't experiment much with shellfish, but such simple flavours go a very long way here.

Ingredients

1 tablespoon minced garlic
1 tablespoon grated ginger
200 g (7 oz) samphire
1 teaspoon chilli paste
1 kg (2 lb 3 oz) pipis
  (or clams), in shell
60 ml (2 fl oz/¼ cup)
  vegetable oil
200 ml (7 fl oz) fish stock
10 g (¼ oz/½ cup) sea
  parsley, chopped
Saltbush and Warrigal
  Greens Damper (page 102),
  to serve

Method

1. In a large frying pan, sauté the garlic, ginger, samphire, chilli paste and pipis over a high heat in the oil until the shells start to open.

2. Add the fish stock, cover the pan with a lid and steam for 10 minutes.

3. Just before serving, toss in the sea parsley.

4. Serve with a good slice of saltbush damper.

Serves 2

Curry Cod

This is a recipe to go with my famous Curry Paste (page 173). This turns out almost like a warm salad – make sure you let it sit for a few hours after cooking, then reheat and eat so the curry is fully integrated. The seablite adds herbaceous saltiness for an extra taste of the ocean.

Ingredients

500 g (1 lb 2 oz) cod
1 large onion, very finely
  diced
2 garlic cloves, crushed
100 g (3½ oz) seablite
5 cm (2 in) piece fresh ginger,
  crushed
1 teaspoon Curry Paste
  (page 173)
pinch of salt
1 tablespoon lime juice
cooked rice, to serve

Method

1. In a large pan, poach the cod in 500 ml (17 fl oz/ 2 cups) boiling water with the onion, garlic, seablite and ginger for about 10 minutes. Set aside to cool.

2. When cool, remove the cod – reserving the broth – and flake apart into chunks.

3. Now stir the fish back into the broth, adding the curry paste, a pinch of salt and the lime juice. Leave to marinate for 2 hours in the fridge.

4. When required, warm the dish on the stove and serve with rice.

Fresh Squid Ragu

This is a rich tomato-based entrée or dip that makes a great start to a meal. The bush tomato adds extra depth of flavour. You can serve this hot or cold with taro chips or fresh bread.

Ingredients

1 kg (2 lb 3 oz) whole squid,
  cut into 2.5 cm (1 in) slices,
  (you can leave the tentacles
  whole if you like)
1 garlic clove, crushed
2 large onions, diced
1 tablespoon vegetable oil
500 g (1 lb 2 oz) very ripe
  roma (plum) tomatoes,
  roughly chopped
pinch of salt
1 tablespoon ground bush
  tomato
4 mint leaves
4 tablespoons tomato paste
  (concentrated purée)
sea saltbush, to garnish
  (optional)
fresh bread or taro chips,
  to serve

Method

1. Boil the squid in a pot of salted water until partly cooked – about 7 minutes.

2. In a large pan, brown the garlic and onion in the oil over a high heat, then add the tomato to the pan with a pinch of salt, the bush tomato and mint leaves. (If you prefer, you can skin the tomatoes before cooking. Pour some boiling water over them, simmer for 10 minutes, then remove the skin before dicing.)

3. Add the squid meat and tomato paste to the tomato sauce and cook, covered, for 45 minutes until tender.

4. Serve garnished with sea saltbush, if using, and with some fresh bread or taro chips.

Tamarind Pipis

The usual way to eat pipis is to place them on a hot plate until they open up, then eat them straight from the shell. This super quick recipe uses tamarind – lots of people don't realise how delicious tamarind is! This is a great way to taste the full flavour of the fruit. Don't be afraid to get your hands dirty here and feel your meal.

Ingredients

300 g (10½ oz) fresh
  tamarind paste
2 onions, diced
2 garlic cloves, crushed
½ tablespoon vegetable oil
1 teaspoon Curry Powder
  (page 173)
½ teaspoon salt
2 kg (4 lb 6 oz) pipis
  (or clams), in shell
500 g (1 lb 2 oz) warrigal
  greens

Method

1. Start by making a tamarind paste by pouring 250 ml (8½ fl oz/1 cup) warm water over the tamarind paste 1 hour before you need it. Hand-mush the paste to get more out of the tamarind juice. Break up the pulp as much as possible with your fingers. Set aside.

2. In a large pan or work, fry the onion and garlic in the oil over a high heat until cooked.

3. Add the curry powder, salt and the pipis. Stir well for a couple of minutes.

4. Strain the tamarind water directly into the pan, discarding the pulp. Add the warrigal greens at the end, cover and steam for 3 minutes.

Smelly-but-yum-using-everything Blatchan

Blatchan or belacan sambal is an intense prawn paste. It is a Malaysian-style ingredient that made its way to the Straits. This is one of those dishes that stinks up the whole house when you're cooking it, but it's so worth it. It's hard on the nose, delicious in the belly.

Ingredients

100 g (3½ oz) chicken kidney
50 g (1¾ oz) chicken giblets
50 g (1¾ oz) duck heart
50 g (1¾ oz) chicken liver
100 g (3½ oz) pipi meat
2 tablespoons vegetable oil
2 onions, diced
2 garlic cloves, crushed
5 cm (2 in) piece fresh ginger,
   crushed
2 bird's eye chillies, finely
   chopped
1 teaspoon prawn paste
30 ml (1 fl oz) white vinegar
cooked rice or fried ripe
   bananas, to serve

Method

1. In a medium pan, fry the kidney, giblets, heart, liver and pipi meat in 1 tablespoon of the oil over a high heat until browned, then chop everything finely and set aside.

2. In the same pan, fry the onion, garlic, ginger and chillies in the remaining oil until cooked.

3. Dissolve the prawn paste in the vinegar and 200 ml (7 fl oz) water.

4. Add the meat and the prawn paste mix to the pan and simmer for a few minutes, adding more water if the mixture starts to dry up.

5. Serve with rice or fried ripe bananas.

Cuttlefish Blatchan

This quick-pickled cuttlefish is another recipe using pungent blatchan prawn paste. It's delicious on a cracker, or you could stir it through a squid ink pasta; the flavours match perfectly.

Ingredients

500 g (1 lb 2 oz) cleaned
   baby cuttlefish
1 level teaspoon prawn paste
40 ml (1¼ fl oz) lime juice
1 spring onion, sliced
   lenghtways
squid ink pasta or crackers,
   to serve
charred limes, to serve

Method

1. Boil the cuttlefish for 20 minutes, then drain and chop the meat finely.

2. Dissolve the prawn paste in the lime juice in a bowl, add the chopped squid and spring onion and let it soak for about 20 minutes.

3. Serve with squid ink pasta or crackers and lime on the side.

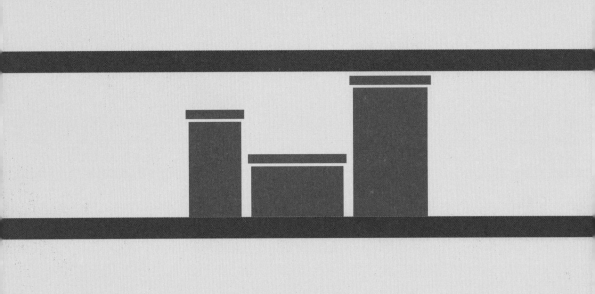

Larder

Golden Syrup Butter

This is the numero uno sweet butter – it's so simple, but just so delicious. Every Island person will spread a thick layer on any slice of damper or scone. Make a batch and keep it in the freezer as you'll keep wanting more.

Ingredients

500 g (1 lb 2 oz/2 cups) unsalted butter, at room temperature

4 tablespoons golden syrup (light treacle)

Method

1. Make sure your butter has a spreadable consistency, but is not too soft. Blend the butter and golden syrup in a food processor until fully whipped, then wrap the butter mix in a large piece of plastic wrap.

2. Holding both ends, roll the wrapped butter into a log.

3. Place in the freezer for 10 minutes to harden before using, then store in the freezer for up to 7 months.

Wattleseed Butter

This has a lovely hazelnutty coffee taste. Use it to add a native flavour to a croissant or fruit toast.

Ingredients

500 g (1 lb 2 oz/2 cups) unsalted butter

1 tablespoon sieved ground wattleseed

100 ml (3½ fl oz) golden syrup (light treacle)

Method

1. Make sure your butter has a spreadable consistency, but is not too soft. Blend all the ingredients in a food processor until fully whipped, then wrap the butter mix in a large piece of plastic wrap.

2. Holding both ends, roll the wrapped butter into a log.

3. Place in the freezer for 10 minutes to harden before using, then store in the freezer for up to 7 months.

Saltbush Butter

This adds a deeply savoury, salty hit to any piece of steak or barbecue meat. These butters offer a lot of bang for buck – they're really easy to prepare, but bring lots of flavour.

Ingredients

500 g (1 lb 2 oz/2 cups)
  unsalted butter
1 tablespoon dried saltbush

Method

1. Make sure your butter has a spreadable consistency, but is not too soft. Blend the butter and saltbush in a food processor until fully whipped, then wrap the butter mix in a large piece of plastic wrap.

2. Holding both ends, roll the wrapped butter into a log.

3. Place in the freezer for 10 minutes to harden before using, then store in the freezer for up to 7 months.

Saltbush and Pepperberry Butter

The native salt and pepper! The saltbush and pepperberry gives a clovey, tasty richness to the butter. You could start a sauce base with a cube of this, or rub it all over your roast chicken before putting it in the oven.

Ingredients

400 g (14 oz) unsalted butter
1 tablespoon saltbush
1 teaspoon ground
  pepperberry

Method

1. Make sure your butter has a spreadable consistency, but is not too soft. Blend all the ingredients in a food processor until fully whipped, then wrap the butter mix in a large piece of plastic wrap.

2. Holding both ends, roll the wrapped butter into a log.

3. Place in the freezer for 10 minutes to harden before using, then store in the freezer for up to 7 months.

Saltbush and Sea Parsley Butter

Finish off your steak with a thick slice of this baby – boom! It's delicious, and shows you can give a native spin to many of your dishes super quickly. It also goes well with fried fish.

Ingredients

1 garlic clove
500 g (1 lb 2 oz/2 cups) unsalted butter
1 teaspoon dried saltbush
2 tablespoons chopped sea parsley
1 tablespoon lemon juice
pinch of white pepper

Method

1. Blanch the garlic in boiling water for 2 minutes, then crush.

2. Make sure your butter has a spreadable consistency, but is not too soft. Cream the butter with the garlic, then add the saltbush, parsley, lemon juice and pepper.

3. Wrap the butter mix in a large piece of plastic wrap.

4. Holding both ends, roll the wrapped butter into a log.

5. Place in the freezer for 10 minutes to harden before using, then store in the freezer for up to 7 months.

Strawberry Gum Cream

This is a nice easy cream that you can add to fresh fruit for a different kind of flavour. The strawberry gum shows you how cool and tasty a leaf can really be.

Ingredients

500 g (1 lb 2 oz) thick (double/heavy) cream, or coconut yoghurt
1 teaspoon ground strawberry gum, or you can use lemon myrtle or cinnamon myrtle
60 g (2 oz/½ cup) icing (confectioners') sugar

Method

1. In a large bowl, mix the cream, strawberry gum and sugar together using a hand-held mixer (or use a stand mixer) and whip until thickened. Be careful not to overmix; this should only take 2 minutes using a machine mixer.

2. Serve on scones, with sweet dampers, fruit and cakes, or on top of a pavlova.

Serves 4–6

Strawberry Gum Ricotta Cream

This also showcases the delicious power of strawberry gum, but the ricotta adds a cheesy richness. This would work really well as an Italian cannoli filling.

Ingredients

1 kg (2 lb 3 oz/4 cups) ricotta
3 tablespoons vanilla extract
250 g (9 oz/2 cups) icing (confectioners') sugar
1 tablespoon ground strawberry gum
600 ml (20½ fl oz) thick (double/heavy) cream
seasonal fruit, to serve

Method

1. In a large bowl, blend the ricotta, vanilla, sugar and strawberry gum using a hand-held mixer (or use a stand mixer) until nice and smooth.

2. Whip the cream until thickened.

3. Fold the ricotta and cream together.

4. Serve with some seasonal fruit.

Curry Powder

This yellow curry powder is so versatile and can be used as a 'master powder' for a lot of other dishes. While my traditional Tin Meat and Rice (page 126) uses Keen's curry powder, this home-made version has plenty of punch and deep flavour. Like it spicier? You can customise it to your own taste.

Ingredients

70 g (2½ oz) ground turmeric
60 g (2 oz) ground coriander
15 g (½ oz) ground ginger
15 g (½ oz) whole
   peppercorns
7 g (⅛ oz) dried bird's
   eye chillies
7 g (⅛ oz) cardamom seeds
12 cloves, ground
50 g (1¾ oz) ground
   caraway seeds

Method

1. Crush all the ingredients together in a food processor or mortar and pestle to make a smooth curry powder.

Curry Paste

This all-purpose curry paste has spiciness from the chillies but also the numbing clove zing from the pepperberries. Their purple tinge will also come through to give this a great colour. It's a wet paste and you can keep it in the fridge for up to a month.

Ingredients

10 bird's eye chillies
1 tablespoon coriander seeds
1 teaspoon salt
40 g (1½ oz) peeled ginger
1 tablespoon lemon myrtle
1 teaspoon ground
   pepperberry
2 tablespoons chopped
   shallots
4 garlic cloves

Method

1. Blend all the ingredients to a smooth paste in a food processor or mortar and pestle and store in a screw-top jar in the refrigerator for up to 1 month.

Pickled Succulents

Karkalla is the ocean cucumber, and you can buy it from many markets. Pickling it is a great way to lock in the flavour, as it will suck up all the other flavours in the jar. You can toss this pickle through salads or add it to a cheese board for a different spin on the grazing platter.

Ingredients

6 cloves star anise
1 tablespoon mustard seeds
5 garlic cloves
1 tablespoon whole
   pepperberries
1 teaspoon whole cloves
250 g (9 oz) caster
   (superfine) sugar
500 ml (17 fl oz/2 cups) white
   vinegar
250 g (9 oz) karkalla
250 g (9 oz) samphire
100 g (3½ oz) seablite

Method

1. In a large saucepan, combine all the spices and the sugar with 1 litre (34 fl oz/4 cups) water and the vinegar, then boil for 15 minutes.

2. Place the sea succulents in sterilised glass jars.

3. Let the pickling juice cool for 3 minutes before adding to the jars.

4. Leave overnight and eat the next day. The pickle will keep for 2 months in the fridge.

Note To sterilise jars, wash them in hot soapy water, then place them in the oven at 110°C (200°F) for about 15 minutes until they are completely dry.

Quandong Relish

The quandong, or wild peach, stands up really well when preserved. It has a similar profile to rhubarb and stews down really nicely. This relish is a great match for any game meat, especially rare kangaroo fillet – it's got a delicious savoury tang.

Ingredients

500 g (1 lb 2 oz) fresh
  quandongs
½ teaspoon ground
  pepperberry
2 tablespoons grated fresh
  ginger
½ teaspoon lemon myrtle
1 teaspoon mustard seeds
5 cardamom pods
300 ml (10 fl oz) malt vinegar
140 g (5 oz) caster (superfine)
  sugar
1 teaspoon salt
2 shallots, diced
1 tablespoon chilli flakes
2 tablespoons ground
  macadamia nuts

Method

1. Add all the ingredients to a pot and simmer for 30 minutes.

2. Remove the cardamom pods and blend the mixture with a hand-held blender until roughly combined.

3. Simmer until the relish is thick and creamy. Store in the fridge in an airtight container for up to 1 month.

My Favourite Chilli Paste

Now, when making paste you need the right chillies, or maybe just your preferred heat on a good chilli. I like to use chilli flakes that give you a nice hot spice in your mouth that opens up the sinuses without leaving a lasting burn.

Ingredients

500 g (1 lb 2 oz) dried red chilli
  flakes (I like Turkish chilli)
1 tablespoon garlic powder
1 tablespoon ginger powder
200 g (7 oz) macadamia nuts
600 ml (20½ fl oz) rice bran oil

Method

1. In a blender, blend the chilli, garlic and ginger powders and macadamia nuts until the macadamias are ground.

2. Place in a bowl and fold through the oil until well mixed. Bottle in sterilised glass jars (see Note on page 175) and you will find yourself having it with everything. This will keep for 4–5 months in the fridge.

Green Tomato Hot Sauce

This is a super versatile hot sauce. It's fresh and zingy and goes well with just about everything: I put it on tacos, serve it with oysters, cooked prawns or even with barbecued lamb.

Ingredients

½ onion, diced

200 g (7 oz) green tomatoes, diced

200 g (7 oz) tomatillo, diced

2 garlic cloves, finely diced

1 jalapeño, finely diced

3 long green chillies, finely diced

50 ml (1¾ fl oz) white vinegar

50 ml (1¾ fl oz) lime juice

30 g (1 oz) desert lime

1 teaspoon salt

¼ bunch of coriander (cilantro), plus the roots, chopped

Method

1. Put the onion, tomato, tomatillo, garlic, jalapeño and chilli in a large pot.

2. Add 50 ml (1¾ fl oz) water, the vinegar, lime juice, desert lime and salt.

3. Cook for 15 minutes, then add the coriander and roots.

4. Blend all the ingredients well using a hand-held blender and bottle straight away in sterilised glass bottles (see Note on page 175). The sauce will keep for up to 2 months in the fridge.

Island Marinade

My dad originally made this marinade when I was growing up and he'd use it on everything! It showcases the mix of Islander and surrounding Asian flavours that appear in Torres Strait Islander cooking. This is a great marinade to use on meats for the barbecue, or you can use it in stir-fries, on roasted chicken, as a dipping sauce or to spice up a good fried rice.

Ingredients

500 ml (17 fl oz/2 cups) soy sauce
50 ml (1¾ fl oz) white vinegar
80 g (2¾ oz/⅓ cup) caster
  (superfine) sugar
50 g (1¾ oz) freshly grated ginger
50 g (1¾ oz) freshly grated garlic

Method

1. Place all the ingredients in a pot and bring to a rolling boil for about 20 minutes.

2. Strain the garlic and ginger from the liquid, then store the marinade in sterilised bottles (see Note on page 175) and use as needed. It will keep for 4–5 months in the fridge.

Molasses Marinade

This is a great molasses mix for making candied bacon or marinating game meats.

Ingredients

150 g (5½ oz) molasses
½ teaspoon ground
  pepperberry
¼ teaspoon saltbush
2 tablespoons brown sugar
2 teaspoons mustard

Method

1. Mix all the ingredients together until the sugar has dissolved.

2. Use it straight away as a marinade on game meats or smoky bacon.

Mabu Sriracha

This sriracha is sweet and spicy without any sugar, getting its sweetness from the carrot, which also gives it a vibrant orange-and-ruby colour.

Ingredients

2 red capsicums (bell peppers)
6 long red chillies
1 habanero chilli
1 large carrot, sliced
2 garlic cloves, sliced
100 ml (3½ fl oz) white vinegar
1 teaspoon sea salt

Method

1. Clean the capsicums and chillies and remove the seeds, then chop roughly and add to a large pot.

2. Add the sliced carrot, garlic, vinegar, salt and 125 ml (4 fl oz/½ cup) water.

3. Cook over a high heat until the carrots and peppers are very soft, about 30 minutes. Add another 60 ml (2 fl oz/¼ cup) water if the mixture becomes too dry.

4. Use a hand-held blender to blend until you have a smooth paste. Store in sterilised glass bottles (see Note on page 175). It will keep for 2 months in the fridge.

Aba's Tea

Aba's tea is named after my grandma, Aba, who loved to wear a hibiscus flower in her hair. It was the first tea I developed for Mabu Mabu. This ruby-red bliss gives you tartness from the lemon myrtle, a deep ruby-red colour from the hibiscus, and a subtle, sweet finish from the strawberry gum and cinnamon myrtle.

Ingredients

200 g (7 oz) dried wild hibiscus

40 g (1½ oz) lemon myrtle leaves

50 g (1¾ oz) cinnamon myrtle leaves

50 g (1¾ oz) strawberry gum leaves

Lemon Myrtle Cookies (page 193), to serve

Method

1. In a bowl, mix all the ingredients until well combined. Store in a jar.

2. Enjoy this loose-leaf tea steeped in hot water, brewed to your liking. The longer you leave it in the water, the more tart it will be. Serve with a lemon myrtle cookie.

Sweets

Fresh Tamarind and Half-ripe Mango

My dad used to send me to confirmation classes as a child. Outside the church, there were these huge tamarind and mango trees, and I would spend most of my time picking the fruit straight off the trees to make my own pickles. I would save up old jars and cram in the tamarinds and slices of green mango, then mix them together with sugar and soy sauce. Then I would share my pickles with whoever wanted to be naughty and skip confirmation classes with me.

Ingredients

Fresh Tamarind

500 g (1 lb 2 oz) fresh tamarind
55 g (2 oz/¼ cup) caster (superfine) sugar, or brown sugar
125 ml (4 fl oz/½ cup) soy sauce

Half-ripe Mango

2 green mangoes
55 g (2 oz/¼ cup) caster (superfine) sugar
125 ml (4 fl oz/½ cup) soy sauce

Method

1. For the tamarind, break open the tamarind and place the flesh in a jar, then add the sugar and soy sauce.

2. Shake really well until the sugar has dissolved.

3. Marinate for 1 hour, then it's ready to eat.

4. For the mangoes, peel and slice the mangoes, then place the slices in a jar. Add the sugar and soy sauce.

5. Shake really well until the sugar has dissolved.

6. Marinate for 1 hour, then they're ready to eat.

Doughboy

Every Island kid loves this as a snack – it's about using all parts of the cassava. Similar to a Domboi (page 91), this recipe uses an old method of extracting cassava starch so it becomes gelatinous. It's similar to the Banana Pakalolo (page 197) in that it needs to be eaten right away before it goes hard.

Ingredients

3 medium-sized cassava, peeled and grated
150 g (5½ oz/1 cup) plain (all-purpose) flour
55 g (2 oz/¼ cup, firmly packed) brown sugar
pinch of salt
600 ml (20½ fl oz) coconut milk

Method

1. Place the grated cassava into a piece of muslin (cheesecloth) and squeeze its juices through the cloth into a bowl. Set aside the flesh and let the juice settle for 30 minutes, then pour away the clear liquid on the top leaving the remaining starch at the bottom of the bowl.

2. Add the flour, sugar, a pinch of salt and the grated cassava to the starch and mix well until combined. Roll the mixture into small balls.

3. Bring the coconut milk to the boil in a medium pot over a high heat and drop the cassava balls into the milk. Reduce the heat to medium and simmer for about 45 minutes, or until cooked.

Wattleseed Caramel Panna Cotta

This classic rich dessert is fantastic, with a bitter chocolate and hazelnut finish from the wattleseed. This is my version of a tiramisu, which I can't eat because I can't have coffee. The honeycomb caramel is delicious, too – a real treat after a meal.

Ingredients

10 g (¼ oz) powdered gelatine
1 vanilla bean
250 ml (8½ fl oz/1 cup) thick (double/heavy) cream
70 g (2½ oz) caster (superfine) sugar

Honeycomb Caramel
1 teaspoon finely ground wattleseed
100 g (3½ oz) caster (superfine) sugar

Method

1. To make the caramel, place the wattleseed and sugar in a small saucepan with 120 ml (4 fl oz) water and cook over a medium heat for 20 minutes, whisking occasionally, until you have a thick caramel sauce. Set aside to completely cool.

2. Activate the gelatine by adding it to 1 tablespoon of water to soften.

3. Slice the vanilla bean in half and scrape out the seeds.

4. Place the cream, gelatine, sugar and the vanilla bean and seeds in a small pot and simmer until the sugar has dissolved.

5. Prepare four ramekins by spraying them with some cooking oil so the panna cotta doesn't stick. Place 1 tablespoon of the caramel in each ramekin, then pour in the panna cotta cream.

6. Set in the fridge for 2 hours before eating. To serve, you can carefully run a knife around the edge of the ramekin to turn out the panna cotta if you like, or serve it in the ramekin.

Makes 350 ml (12 fl oz)

Desert Lime Syrup

This is the perfect vehicle for the desert lime, which is a way underrated lime. You're making your own unique cordial here, and adding fresh river mint makes it extra refreshing with the citrus tang. You can add the syrup to cream, pour it over ice cream, or use it to make a different style of lime tart.

Ingredients

200 g (7 oz) desert limes
2 cardamom pods, bruised
100 g (3½ oz) caster (superfine) sugar
100 ml (3½ fl oz) lime juice
50 ml (1¾ fl oz) lemon juice
crushed ice, soda water (club soda) and fresh river mint sprigs, to serve

Method

1. Place the desert limes, cardamom, sugar, lime and lemon juice in a large pot.

2. Cook over a high heat for 30 minutes, stirring regularly, until you get a thick syrup.

3. Set aside to cool, pour into sterilised bottles (see Note on page 175) and store overnight in the fridge, then it's ready to use. This will keep for 4–5 months in the fridge.

4. Serve 30 ml (1 fl oz) syrup with crushed ice, soda water and a sprig of fresh river mint.

Lemon Myrtle Cookies

This is a brilliant butter cookie with a zesty lemon myrtle finish. You'll get that amazing lemon flavour without having to use lemons. Just try and stop after eating one!

Ingredients

225 g (8 oz) butter,
   at room temperature
225 g (8 oz) caster
   (superfine) sugar
1 tablespoon vanilla extract
3 eggs
350 g (12½ oz/2⅓ cups)
   self-raising flour, sifted
   (see Note on page 99)
20 g (¾ oz) ground
   lemon myrtle
1 teaspoon poppy seeds

Method

1. Preheat the oven to 170°C (340°F) and line a baking tray with baking paper.

2. Whisk the butter, sugar and vanilla in a bowl until creamy.

3. Add one egg at a time, mixing until combined.

4. In a separate bowl, mix together the flour, ground lemon myrtle and poppy seeds.

5. Fold the wet mix into the dry mix.

6. Roll into small balls, about 1 tablespoon of mixture each.

7. Place the balls on the baking paper and press each one down with a fork.

8. Bake for 15–20 minutes. These are great with a cup of Aba's Tea (page 183).

Hibiscus and Quandong Frangipani Cake

This traditional frangipani cake with a native twist would go down a treat at afternoon tea-time with a cuppa. The hibiscus has a beautiful ruby-red colour, and the quandongs work in a similar way to rhubarb.

Ingredients

150 g (5½ oz) butter, plus extra for greasing
1 teaspoon vanilla extract
165 g (6 oz/¾ cup) sugar
3 large eggs
150 g (5½ oz/1 cup) plain (all-purpose) flour
100 g (3½ oz/1 cup) ground almonds
½ teaspoon baking powder
15 g (½ oz/⅓ cup) dried hibiscus flowers, plus extra to decorate
400 g (14 oz/1½ cups) quandongs, halved and deseeded
1 tablespoon icing (confectioners') sugar

Method

1. Preheat the oven to 170°C (340°F).

2. Grease a 22 cm (8¾ in) round cake or flan (tart) tin and line the bottom with baking paper.

3. With an electric mixer, beat the butter, vanilla extract and sugar in a bowl until fluffy, mixing well for at least 5 minutes. Add one egg at a time until all mixed in.

4. In a separate bowl, mix together the flour, ground almonds and baking powder.

5. Add the dry mix to the wet mix and beat until just combined. Fold in the dried hibiscus and quandongs until well mixed in. Transfer to the cake tin.

6. Bake for 35 minutes, or until golden and a cake skewer inserted in the centre comes out clean.

7. Set to one side to cool completely.

8. Mix some extra ground hibiscus with the icing sugar and dust the cooled cake to finish.

Makes 1 kg (2 lb 3 oz)
or 3–4 jars

Quick Lemon Myrtle Jam

A 20-minute jam is an ideal way to use up all sorts of seasonal fruits. Don't be afraid to experiment here, but the lemon myrtle is a must-include. Lemon myrtle really loves sugar.

Ingredients

500 g (1 lb 2 oz) blueberries
500 g (1 lb 2 oz/3⅓ cups)
  strawberries, hulled
200 g (7 oz) caster
  (superfine) sugar
50 g (1¾ oz) ground
  lemon myrtle
300 ml (10 fl oz) apple juice

Method

1. Put all the ingredients in a pot and place over a high heat until boiling, then lower the temperature to a simmer until the mixture has thickened, about 30 minutes, making sure to stir every now and then to stop the mixture sticking to the side of the pot.

2. To check if your jam is ready, place a dollop on a small plate and place it in the fridge for 5 minutes. If the jam is still runny, it needs a little longer on the stove.

3. Wait until the jam is cooled and store in sterilised jars (see Note on page 175) in the fridge for up to 4 months. Serve with wattleseed scones, on damper, or drizzled on top of pavlova.

Serves 6

Coconut Panna Cotta

You want to make sure you use the right combination of coconut milk and cream here – I use Kara brand. The coconut cream adds extra thickness and body to the coconut milk for a rich, delicious dessert. This is the perfect side to my Banana Pakalolo (page 197, both pictured).

Ingredients

10 g (¼ oz) powdered
  gelatine
500 ml (17 fl oz/2 cups)
  coconut milk
250 ml (8½ fl oz/1 cup)
  coconut cream
55 g (2 oz/¼ cup) caster
  (superfine) sugar
fruit of choice, to garnish
  (optional)

Method

1. Activate the gelatine by adding it to 1 tablespoon water to soften.

2. Place all the ingredients in a small saucepan and simmer until the sugar is completely dissolved. Set aside.

3. Prepare six ramekins by spraying them with some cooking oil so the panna cotta doesn't stick.

4. Pour the mixture into the ramekins, cover and place in the fridge for 2 hours. To serve, run a knife around the edge of the ramekin to turn out the panna cotta, or serve it in the ramekin, garnished with fruit if you like.

Serves 10–12

Banana Pakalolo

I made this dish on *MasterChef* in 2021. It's a typical Island celebration dish, which shows how traditional ingredients, such as cassava, can really shine. Pakalolo is loved by all Torres Strait Islanders and was once a big staple but is now rarely made because it's quite time-consuming. But I want to change that! It's a sticky pudding–style treat that needs to be eaten straight away, and is absolutely worth the effort – especially when it's served with my Coconut Panna Cotta (page 195).

Ingredients

2 kg (4 lb 6 oz) cassava, peeled and grated
55 g (2 oz/¼ cup) caster (superfine) sugar
¼ teaspoon lemon myrtle
3 ripe bananas, mashed
75 g (2¾ oz/½ cup) plain (all-purpose) flour
2 × 50 cm (19¾ in) banana leaves (see Note on page 99)
800 ml (27 fl oz) thick coconut milk
100 g (3½ oz) plain (all-purpose) flour
1 teaspoon ground cinnamon myrtle
700 ml (23½ fl oz) vegetable oil

Method

1. Place the cassava pulp in a piece of muslin (cheesecloth) and add 60 ml (2 fl oz/¼ cup) water. Squeeze out all the liquid into a bowl, reserving the pulp. Let it stand until the liquid has settled and the water has cleared. Drain the liquid to reveal the remaining starch.

2. Add your starch and leftover pulp to a bowl with the sugar, lemon myrtle, banana and flour, and mix well.

3. Before using your banana leaves, you need to release the oils to make them flexible and bring out the flavours. Hold the banana leaves over an open gas flame and move them across the flame in sections until the oils seep through the entire leaf. If you do not have a gas flame, place in a dry non-stick frying pan for a few seconds on each side.

4. Place the mixture in the centre of the double-layered banana leaves. Wrap it, folding over each end, and roll it up like a burrito. Then wrap in aluminium foil using the same method.

5. Bake in the oven at 180°C (360°F) for 1 hour and 15 minutes until the cassava is sticky.

6. Remove the banana leaves, put the hot cassava mixture in a bowl and pour the coconut milk over. Mix well with two wooden spoons so the coconut milk combines with the cassava mixture.

7. Combine the flour and cinnamon myrtle. Roll the cassava mix into 10–12 doughnut shapes and dust it in the flour mixture. Heat the oil in a large frying pan over a high heat and shallow-fry the pakalolo for about 2 minutes, or until crispy. Serve warm.

Quandong Christmas Cake

There's no better way to celebrate the end of the year than with this perfect Christmas cake. It's super simple: you boil everything down, and the native ingredients add so much punch. This is the cake I make every year and people love it. It celebrates our Australian nuts, muntries, quandongs and spices such as pepperberries. It's really got everything, and it's the easiest Christmas cake you're ever going to make.

Ingredients

250 g (9 oz/1 cup) butter,
  plus extra for greasing
100 g (3½ oz) brown sugar
3 tablespoons golden syrup
  (light treacle)
100 g (3½ oz) dried
  cranberries
200 g (7 oz) fresh quandongs
75 g (2¾ oz) macadamia
  nuts, chopped
125 ml (4 fl oz/½ cup) brandy
200 g (7 oz/1⅓ cups) currants
200 g (7 oz) muntries
1 tablespoon ground
  cinnamon myrtle
1 tablespoon ground allspice
1 tablespoon baking powder
1 tablespoon ground
  strawberry gum
1 teaspoon ground
  pepperberry
1 teaspoon lemon zest
220 g (8 oz) plain
  (all-purpose) flour
50 g (1¾ oz/⅓ cup)
  self-raising flour (see Note
  on page 99)
1½ teaspoons bicarbonate of
  soda (baking soda)
2 eggs, lightly beaten
Strawberry Gum Cream
  (page 172), to serve

Method

1. Preheat the oven to 160°C (320°F).

2. In a large pot, simmer the butter, brown sugar, golden syrup, cranberries, quandongs, macadamias, brandy, currants and muntries with 200 ml (7 fl oz) water until the sugar has dissolved and the fruit has softened.

3. Set aside for 10 minutes to let the mixture cool. Butter a 20–23 cm (8–9 in) round cake tin and line with baking paper.

4. Add the spices and lemon zest to the flours, along with the bicarbonate of soda, and mix in well.

5. Add the eggs to the cooled fruit mixture, then mix in the spiced flour until well combined. Pour the mix into the prepared cake tin.

6. Bake for 1 hour 25 minutes. Around the 45-minute mark, place a sheet of aluminium foil on top to make sure the top of your cake does not blacken or dry out.

7. Serve with strawberry gum cream.

Index

Thank You

Firstly, I'd like to say au wa esso (biggest thank you) to my father, George Gai Bero, who gave me a name I will always have to spell out. I carry the strong culture and all your dreams with me always, which guides me in life. Thank you for all the dreaming and never giving up, and for all the jokes and the singalongs – my Black Elvis.

To my beautiful wife, Charlie, thank you for always being my rock and for always fighting for what is right in this world. Also, for all the taste-tests you have done, my condiment queen. You have been a huge part of this book coming together and in getting me to the end of the line. Thank you for always being the most colourful person in the room – my stingray forever, xx.

Thank you to Hugo for being the very best friend someone could have. We have been eating our way through all the challenges. Thank you for sharing this business with me. This book is both of us – my brother from another mother.

A special thank you to Anna and Jane from Hardie Grant for giving me this opportunity and sticking with me all the way. And thank you to the rest of the team for making it all come together. It's one of the coolest things I've ever done.

Mabu Mabu

About the Author

Nornie Bero is from the Meriam People of Mer Island in the Torres Strait and is the Executive Chef, CEO and Owner of Mabu Mabu. Bero has been a professional chef for more than twenty-five years. Her style of cooking is all about generosity and flavour and she has been creating dishes using Australian native ingredients for much of her career. Mabu Mabu's venues – Tuckshop in Yarraville, and Big Esso in Federation Square, Melbourne, champion Islander flavours and Australian native produce. Through the business and this book, Nornie is on a mission to make Indigenous herbs, spices, vegetables and fruits a part of everyone's kitchen pantry.

Published in 2022 by Hardie Grant Books,
an imprint of Hardie Grant Publishing

Hardie Grant Books (Melbourne)
Wurundjeri Country
Building 1, 658 Church Street
Richmond, Victoria 3121

Hardie Grant Books (London)
5th & 6th Floors
52–54 Southwark Street
London SE1 1UN

hardiegrantbooks.com

Hardie Grant acknowledges the Traditional Owners of the country on which we work, the Wurundjeri people of the Kulin nation and the Gadigal people of the Eora nation, and recognises their continuing connection to the land, waters and culture. We pay our respects to their Elders past, present and emerging.

A catalogue record for this book is available from the National Library of Australia

Mabu Mabu

ISBN 9781 74379 728 0

10 9 8 7 6 5 4 3 2 1

Publishing Director: Jane Willson
Project Editor: Anna Collett
Writer: Michael Harry
Editor: Andrea O'Connor
Design Manager: Kristin Thomas
Designer: George Saad
Photographer: Armelle Habib
Stylist: Lee Blaylock
Production Manager: Todd Rechner
Production Coordinator: Jessica Harvie

Colour reproduction by Splitting Image Colour Studio
Printed in China by Leo Paper Products LTD.

The paper this book is printed on is from FSC®-certified forests and other sources. FSC® promotes environmentally responsible, socially beneficial and economically viable management of the world's forests.